The Free Gift of God

C. H. Spurgeon on Salvation

Charles H. Spurgeon

Bibliographic Information

Charles H. Spurgeon (1834–1892), affectionately known by many as "the Prince of Preachers," addressed more than 10 million people during his ministry, baptized thousands of converts, and wrote so extensively and persuasively that his sermons have sold more than 50 million copies worldwide. Spurgeon's sermons were initially published in 1855 in a multi-volume series known as *The New Park Street Pulpit*. Spelling, grammar, and punctuation have been gently updated.

an Ichthus Publications *edition*

Copyright © 2015 Ichthus Publications
ISBN 13: 978-1511526654
ISBN 10: 1511526653

www.ichthuspublications.com

CONTENTS

1

Salvation of the Lord[1]

"Salvation is of the Lord" (Jonah 2:9).

JONAH LEARNED THIS SENTENCE of good theology in a strange college. He learned it in the whale's belly, at the bottom of the mountains, with the weeds wrapped about his head, when he supposed that the earth with her bars was about him forever. Most of the grand truths of God have to be learned by trouble; they must be burned into us with the hot iron of affliction, otherwise we shall not truly receive them. No man is competent to judge in matters of the kingdom, until first he has been tried; since there are many things to be learned in the depths which we can never know in the heights. We discover many secrets in the caverns of the ocean, which, though we had soared to Heaven, we never could have known. He shall best meet the wants of God's people as a preacher who has had those wants himself; he shall best comfort God's Israel who has needed comfort; and he shall best preach salvation who has felt his own need of it. Jonah, when he was delivered from his great danger, when, by the command of God the fish had

---

[1] A sermon delivered by C. H. Spurgeon on May 10, 1857 at the Music Hall, Royal Surrey Gardens.

obediently left its great deeps and delivered its cargo upon dry land, was then capable of judging; and this was the result of his experience under his trouble—"Salvation is of the Lord."

By *salvation* here we do not merely understand the special salvation which Jonah received from death; for according to Dr. Gill, there is something so special in the original, in the word *salvation* having one more letter than it usually has, when it only refers to some temporary deliverance, that we can only understand it here as relating to the great work of the salvation of the soul which endures forever. That "salvation is of the Lord," I shall this morning try to show as best I can. First, I shall endeavor to explain the doctrine; then I shall try to show you how God has guarded us from making any mistakes, and has hedged us up to make us believe the Gospel; then I shall dwell upon the influence of this truth upon men; and shall close up by showing you the counterpart of the doctrine. Seeing every truth hath its obverse, so, too, do this.

AN EXPLANATION OF THE DOCTRINE

First, then, to begin by explanation, let us expound this doctrine— the doctrine that Salvation is of the Lord, or of Jehovah. We are to understand by this, that the whole of the work whereby men are saved from their natural estate of sin and ruin, and are translated into the Kingdom of God and made heirs of eternal happiness, is of God, and of Him only. "Salvation is of the Lord."

To begin, then, at the beginning, the plan of salvation is entirely of God. No human intellect and no created intelligence assisted God in the planning of salvation; He contrived the way, even as He Himself carried it out. The plan of salvation was devised before the existence of angels. Before the day-star flung its ray across the darkness, when as yet the unnavigated ether had not been fanned by the wing of seraph, and when the solemnity of silence had never been disturbed by the song of angel, God had devised a way whereby He might save man, whom He foresaw would fall. He did not create angels to consult with them; no, of Himself He did it.

We might truly ask the question, "With whom took He counsel? Who instructed Him, when be planned the great architecture of the temple of mercy? With whom took He counsel when He digged the depths of love, that out of them there might well up springs of salvation? Who aided Him?"

None.

He Himself, alone, did it. In fact, if angels had then been in existence, they could not have assisted God; for I can well suppose that if a solemn conclave of those spirits had been held, if God had put to them this question, "Man will rebel; I declare I will punish; my justice, inflexible and severe, demands that I should do so; but yet I intend to have mercy;" if He had put the question to the celestial squadrons of mighty ones, "How can those things be? How can justice have its demands fulfilled, and how can mercy reign?"

The angels would have sat in silence until now; they could not have dictated the plan; it would have surpassed angelic intellect to have conceived the way whereby righteousness and peace should meet together, and judgment and mercy should kiss each other. God devised it, because without God it could not have been devised. It is a plan too splendid to have been the product of *any* mind except of that mind which afterward carried it out. "Salvation" is older than creation; it is "of the Lord."

And as it was of the Lord in planning so it was of the Lord in execution. No one has helped to provide salvation; God has done it all Himself. The banquet of mercy is served up by one host; that host is He to whom the cattle on a thousand hills belong. But none have contributed any dainties to that royal banquet; He has done it all Himself. The royal bath of mercy, wherein black souls are washed, was filled from the veins of Jesus; not a drop was contributed by any other being. He died upon the cross, and as an Expiator He died alone. No blood of martyrs mingled with that stream; no blood of noble confessors and of heroes of the cross entered into the river of atonement; that is filled from the veins of Christ, and from nowhere else beside. He has done it wholly. Atonement is the unaided work of Jesus.

On yonder cross I see the man who "trod the winepress alone;" in yonder garden I see the solitary conqueror, who came to the fight single-handed, whose own arm brought salvation, and whose omnipotence sustained Him. "Salvation is of the Lord," as to its provisions; Jehovah—Father, Son, and Spirit—hath provided everything.

So far we are all agreed: but now we shall have to separate a bit. "Salvation is of the Lord" in the application of it.

"No," says the Arminian, "it is not; salvation is of the Lord, inasmuch as He does all for man that He can do; but there is something that man must do, which if he does not do, he must perish."

That is the Arminian way of salvation. Now last week I thought of this very theory of salvation, when I stood by the side of that window of Carisbrooke castle, out of which King Charles of unhappy and unrighteous memory, attempted to escape. I read in the guide book that everything was provided for his escape; his followers had means at the bottom of the wall to enable him to fly across the country, and on the coast they had their boats lying ready to take him to another land; in fact everything was ready for his escape. But here was the important circumstance: his friends had done all they could; he was to do the rest; but that doing the rest was just the point and brunt of the battle. It was to get out of the window, out of which he was not able to escape by any means, so that all his friends did for him went for nothing, so far as he was concerned. So it is with the sinner. If God had provided every means of escape, and only required him to get out of his dungeon, he would have remained there to all eternity.

Why, is not the sinner by nature dead in sin? And if God requires him to make himself alive, and then afterward He will do the rest for him, then verily, my friends, we are not so much obliged to God as we had thought for; for if He require so much as that of us, and we can do it, we can do the rest without His assistance.

The Romanists have an extraordinary miracle of their own about St. Dennis, of whom they tell the lying legend that after his head was off be took it up in his hands and walked with it two thousand miles; whereupon, said a wit, "So far as the two thousand miles go, it is nothing at all; it is only the first step in which there is any difficulty."

So I believe, if that is taken, all the rest can be easily accomplished. And if God does require of the sinner—dead in sin—that he should take the first step, then He requireth just that which renders salvation as impossible under the Gospel as ever it was under the Law, seeing man is as unable to believe as he is to obey, and is just as much without power to come to Christ as he is without power to go to Heaven without Christ. The power must be given to him of the Spirit. He lieth dead in sin; the Spirit must quicken him. He is bound hand and foot and fettered by transgression; the Spirit must cut his bonds, and then he will leap to liberty. God must come and dash the iron bars out of their sockets, and then he can escape from the window, and make good his escape afterward; but unless the first thing be done for him, he must perish as surely under the Gospel as he would have done under the Law.

I would cease to preach if I believed that God, in the matter of salvation, required anything whatever of man which He Himself had not also engaged to furnish. For how many have I frequently hanging upon my lips of the worst of characters—men whose lives have become so

11

horribly bad, that the lip of morality would refuse to give a description of their character? When I enter my pulpit am I to believe that these men are to do something before God's Spirit will operate upon them? If so, I should go there with a faint heart, feeling that I never could induce them to do the first part. But now I come to my pulpit with a sure confidence— God the Holy Spirit will meet with these men this morning. They are as bad as they can be; He will put a new thought into their hearts; He will give them new wishes; He will give them new wills, and those who hated Christ will desire to love Him; those who once loved sin will, by God's Divine Spirit, be made to hate it; and here is my confidence, that what they cannot do, in that they are weak through the flesh, God sending His Spirit into their hearts will do for them, and in them, and so they shall be saved.

Well then, says one, that will make people sit still and fold their arms. Sir, it shall not. But if men did so I could not help it; my business, as I have often said in this place before, is not to prove to you the reasonableness of any truth, nor to defend any truth from its consequences; all I do here, and I mean to keep to it, is just to assert the truth, because it is in the Bible; then, if you do not like it, you must settle the quarrel with my Master, and if you think it unreasonable, you must quarrel with the Bible. Let others defend Scripture and prove it to be true; they can do their work better than I could; mine is just the mere work of proclaiming. I am the messenger; I tell the Master's message; if you do not like the message, quarrel with the Bible, not with me; so long as I have Scripture on my side I will dare and defy you to do anything against me. "Salvation is of the Lord." The Lord has to apply it, to make the unwilling willing, to make the ungodly godly, and bring the vile rebel to the feet of Jesus, or else salvation will never be accomplished. Leave that one thing undone, and you have broken the link of the chain, the very link which was just necessary to its integrity. Take away the fact that God begins the good work, and that He sends us what the old divines call *preventing grace*—take that away, and you have spoilt the whole of salvation; you have just taken the key-stone out of the arch, and down it tumbles. There is nothing left then.

And now on the next point we shall a little disagree again, "Salvation is of the Lord," as to the sustaining of the work in any man's heart. When a man is made a child of God he does not have a stock of grace given to him with which to go on forever, but he has grace for that day; and he must have grace for the next day, and grace for the next, and grace for the next, until days shall end, or else the beginning shall be of no avail. As a man does not make himself spiritually alive, so neither can he keep himself so. He can feed on spiritual food, and so preserve his spiritual strength; he can walk in the commandments of the Lord, and so enjoy rest and peace, but still the inner life is dependent upon the Spirit as much for its after existence as for its first begetting. I do verily believe that if it should ever be my lot to put my foot upon the golden threshold of Paradise, and put this thumb upon the pearly latch, I should never cross the threshold unless I had grace given me to take that last step whereby I might enter Heaven. No man of himself, even when converted, hath any power, except as that power is daily, constantly, and perpetually infused into him by the Spirit. But Christians often set up for independent gentlemen; they get a little stock of Grace in hand, and they say, "My mountain standeth firm, I shall never be moved." But ah! It is not long before the manna begins to be putrid. It was only meant to be the manna for the day, and we have kept it for the morrow, and, therefore, it fails us. We must have fresh Grace.

> "For day by day the manna fell;
> O to learn that lesson well."

So look day by day for fresh grace. Frequently, too, the Christian wants to have grace enough for a month granted to him in one moment. "Oh!" he says, "what a host of troubles I have coming—how shall I meet them all? Oh! That I had grace enough to bear me through them all!"

My dear Friends, you will have Grace enough for your troubles, as they come one by one. "As thy days, so shall thy strength be;" but thy strength shall never be as thy months, or as thy weeks. Thou shalt have thy strength as thou hast thy bread. "Give us this day our daily bread." Give us this day our daily Grace. But why is it you will be troubling yourself about the things of tomorrow?

The common people say, "Cross a bridge when you come to it." That is good advice. Do the same. When a trouble comes, attack it, and down with it, and master it; but do not begin now to forestall your woes.

"Ah! But I have so many," says one. Therefore, I say, do not look further before thee than thou needest. "Sufficient unto the day is the evil thereof." Do as the brave Grecian did, who, when he defended his country from Persia, did not go into the plains to fight, but stood in the narrow pass of Thermopylae; there, when the myriads came to him, they had to come one by one, and he felled them to the earth. Had he ventured into the plain he would have been soon devoured, and his handful would have been melted like a drop of dew in the sea. Stand in the narrow pass of today, and fight thy troubles one by one; but do not rush into the plains of tomorrow, for there thou wilt be routed and killed. As the evil is sufficient so will the grace be. "Salvation is of the Lord."

But, lastly, upon this point. The ultimate perfection of salvation is of the Lord. Soon, soon, the saints of earth shall be saints in light; their hairs of snowy age shall be crowned with perpetual joy and everlasting youth; their eyes suffused with tears shall be made bright as stars, never to be clouded again by sorrow; their hearts that tremble now are to be made joyous and fast, and set forever like pillars in the temple of God. Their follies, their burdens, their griefs, their woes, are soon to be over; sin is to be slain, corruption is to be removed, and a Heaven of spotless purity and of unmingled peace is to be theirs forever. But it must still be by grace. As was the foundation such must the top-stone be; that which laid on earth the first beginning must lay in Heaven the top-most stone. As they were redeemed from their filthy conversation by Grace, so they must be redeemed from death and the grave by Grace too, and they must enter Heaven singing,

> "Salvation of the Lord alone;
> Grace is a shoreless sea."

There may be Arminians here, but they will not be Arminians there; they may here say, "It is of the will of the flesh," but in Heaven they shall not think so. Here they may ascribe some little to the creature; but there they shall cast their crowns at the Redeemer's feet, and acknowledge that he did it all. Here they may sometimes look a little at themselves, and boast somewhat of their own strength; but there, "Not unto us, not unto us," shall be sung with deeper sincerity and with more profound emphasis than they have even sung it here below. In Heaven, when Grace shall have done its work, this truth shall stand out in blazing letters of gold, "Salvation is of the Lord."

HOW GOD HAS HEDGED THIS GOSPEL ABOUT

Thus I have tried to expound the Gospel. Now I shall show you *how God has hedged this Gospel about.*

Some have said salvation in some cases is the result of natural temperament. Well, Sir, well; God has effectually answered your argument. You say that some people are saved because they are naturally religious and inclined to be good; unfortunately I have never met with any of that class of persons yet; but I will suppose for a moment that there are such people. God has unanswerably met your objection; for, strange to say, the great number of these who are saved are just the most unlikely people in the world to have been saved, while a great number of those who perish were once just the very people whom, if natural disposition had anything to do with it, we should have expected to see in Heaven.

Why, there is one here who in his youth was a child of many follies. Often did his mother weep over him, and cry and groan over her son's wanderings; for what with a fierce high spirit that could brook neither bit nor bridle, what with perpetual rebellions and ebullitions of hot anger, she said, "My son, my son, what wilt thou be in thy riper years? Surely thou wilt dash in pieces law and order, and be a disgrace to thy father's name."

He grew up; in youth he was wild and wanton, but, wonder of wonders, on a sudden he became a new man, changed, altogether changed; no more like what he was before than angels are like lost spirits. He sat at her feet, he cheered her heart, and the lost, fiery one became gentle, mild, humble as a little child, and obedient to God's commandments.

You say, wonder of wonders! But there is another here. He was a fair youth: when but a child be talked of Jesus; often when his mother had him on her knee he asked her questions about Heaven; he was a prodigy, a wonder of piety in his youth. As he grew up, the tear rolled down his cheek under any sermon; he could scarcely bear to hear of death without a sigh; sometimes his mother caught him, as she thought, in prayer alone. And what is he now? He has just this very morning come from sin; he has become the debauched desperate villain, has gone far into all manner of wickedness and lust, and sin, and has become more damnably corrupt than other men could have made him only his own evil spirit, once confined, has now developed itself; he has learned to play the lion in his manhood, as once he played the fox in his youth.

I do not know whether you have ever met with such a case; but it very frequently is so. I know I can say that in my congregation some abandoned wicked fellow has had his heart broken, and been led to weep, and has cried to God for mercy, and renounced his vile sin; whilst some fair maiden by his side hath heard the same sermon, and if there was a tear she brushed it away; she still continues just what she was, "without God and without hope in the world." God has taken the base things of the world, and has just picked his people out of the very roughest of men, in order that he may prove that it is not natural disposition, but that "salvation is of the Lord" alone.

Well, but some say, it is the minister they hear who converts men. Ah! That is a grand idea, full sure. No man but a fool would entertain it. I met with a man some time ago who assured me that he knew a minister who had a very large amount of converting power in him. Speaking of a great evangelist in America, he said, "That man, sir, has got the greatest quantity of converting power I ever knew a man to have; and Mr. so-and-so in a neighboring town I think is second to him." At that time this converting power was being exhibited; two hundred persons were converted by the converting power of this second best, and joined to the church in a few months. I went to the place sometime afterwards—it was in England—and I said, "How do your converts get on?"

"Well," said he, "I cannot say much about them."

"How many out of those two hundred whom you received in a year ago stand fast?"

"Well," he said, "I am afraid not many of them; we have turned seventy of them out for drunkenness already."

"Yes," I said, "I thought so: that is the end of the grand experiment of converting power." If I could convert you all, anyone else might unconvert you; what any man can do another man can undo; it is only what God does that is abiding.

No, my brethren; God has taken good care it shall never be said conversion is of man, for usually He blesses those who seem to be the most unlikely to be useful. I do not expect to see so many conversions in this place as I had a year ago, when I had far fewer hearers. Do you ask why? Why, a year ago I was abused by everybody; to mention my name was to mention the name of the most abominable buffoon that lived. The mere utterance of it brought forth oaths and cursing; with many men it was a name of contempt, kicked about the street as a football; but then God gave me souls by hundreds, who were added to my church, and in one year it was my happiness to see not less than a thousand personally who had then been converted. I do not expect that now.

My name is somewhat esteemed now, and the great ones of the earth think it no dishonor to sit at my feet; but this makes me fear lest my God should forsake me now that the world esteems me. I would rather be despised and slandered than aught else. This assembly that you think so grand and fine, I would readily part with, if by such a loss I could gain a greater blessing. "God has chosen the base things of the world;" and, therefore, I reckon that the more esteemed I may be, the worse is my position, so much the less expectation shall I have that God will bless me.

He hath but his treasure in earthen vessels, that the excellency of the power may be of God, and not of man. A poor minister began to preach once, and all the world spoke ill of him; but God blessed him. By-and-bye they turned round and petted him. He was the man—a wonder! God left him! It has often been the same. It is for us to recollect, in all times of popularity, that "Crucify him; crucify him" follows fast upon the heels of

"Hosanna," and that the crowd today, if dealt faithfully with, may turn into the handful of tomorrow; for men love not plain speaking.

We should learn to be despised, learn to be contemned, learn to be slandered, and then we shall learn to be made useful by God. Down on my knees I have often fallen, with the hot sweat rising from my brow, under some fresh slander poured upon me; in an agony of grief my heart has been well-nigh broken; till at last I learned the art of bearing all and caring for none. And how my grief runneth in another line. It is just the opposite. I fear lest God should forsake me, to prove that he is the author of salvation, that it is not in the preacher, that it is not in the crowd, that it is not in the attention I can attract, but in God, and in God alone.

And this thing I hope I can say from my heart: if to be made as the mire of the streets again, if to be the laughingstock of fools and the song of the drunkard once more will make me more serviceable to my Master, and more useful to his cause, I will prefer it to all this multitude, or to all the applause that man could give. Pray for me, dear Friends, pray for me, that God would still make me the means of the salvation of souls; for I fear he may say, "I will not help that man, lest the world should say he has done it," for "salvation is of the Lord," and so it must be, even to the world's end.

THE INFLUENCE OF SALVATION BY GRACE

And now *what is* and *what should be the influence of this doctrine* upon men?

Why, first, with sinners, this doctrine is a great battering ram against their pride. I will give you a figure. The sinner in his natural estate reminds me of a man who has a strong and well-nigh impenetrable castle into which he has fled. There is the outer moat; there is a second moat; there are the high walls; and then afterward there is the dungeon and keep, into which the sinner will retire. Now, the first moat that goes round the sinner's trusting place is his good works. "Ah!" he says, "I am as good as my neighbor; twenty shillings in the pound down, ready money, I have always paid; I am no sinner; 'I tithe mint and cummin;' a good respectable gentleman I am indeed."

Well, when God comes to work with him, to save him, he sends his army across the first moat; and as they go through it, they cry, "Salvation is of the Lord;" and the moat is dried up, for if it be of the Lord, how can it be of good works? But when that is done, he has a second entrenchment—ceremonies. "Well," he says, "I will not trust in my good works, but I have been baptized, I have been confirmed; do not I take the sacrament? That shall be my trust." "Over the moat! Over the moat!" And the soldiers go over again, shouting, "Salvation is of the Lord." The second moat is dried up; it is all over with that.

Now they come to the next strong wall; the sinner, looking over it, says, "I can repent, I can believe, whenever I like; I will save myself by repenting and believing." Up come the soldiers of God, his great army of conviction, and they batter this wall to the ground, crying, " 'Salvation is of the Lord.' Your faith and your repentance must all be given you, or else you will neither believe nor repent of sin." And now the castle is taken; the man's hopes are all cut off; he feels that it is not of self; the castle of self is overcome, and the great banner upon which is written: "Salvation is of the Lord" is displayed upon the battlements.

But is the battle over? Oh no; the sinner has retired to the keep, in the center of the castle; and now he changes his tactics. "I cannot save myself," says he, "Therefore I will despair; there is no salvation for me." Now this second castle is as hard to take as the first, for the sinner sits down and says, "I can't be saved, I must perish." But God commands the soldiers to take this castle, too, shouting, "Salvation is of the Lord;" though it is not of man, it is of God; "he is able to save, even to the uttermost," though you cannot save yourself. This sword, you see, cuts two ways; it cut pride down, and then it cleaves the skull of despair. If any man say he can save himself, it halveth his pride at once; and if another man say he cannot be saved, it dasheth his despair to the earth; for it affirms that he can be saved, seeing, "Salvation is of the Lord." That is the effect this doctrine has upon the sinner, may it have that effect on you!

But what influence has it upon the saint? Why, it is the keystone of all divinity. I will defy you to be heterodox if you believe this truth. You must be sound in the faith if you have learned to spell this sentence— "Salvation is of the Lord;" and if you feel it in your soul you will not be proud; you cannot be; you will cast everything at his feet, confessing that you have done nothing, save what He has helped you to do and therefore the glory must be where the salvation is. If you believe this you will not be distrustful. You will say, "My salvation does not depend on my faith, but on the Lord; my keeping does not depend on myself, but on God who keepeth me; my being brought to Heaven rests not now in my own hands, but in the hands of God;" you will, when doubts and fears prevail, fold your arms, look upward and say,

"And now my eye of faith is dim,
I trust in Jesus, sink or swim."

If you can keep this in your mind you may always be joyful. He can have no cause for trouble who knows and feels that his salvation is of God. Come on, legions of Hell; come on demons of the pit!

"He that has helped me bears me through,
And makes me more than conqueror too."

21

Salvation resteth not on this poor arm, else should I despair, but on the arm of the Omnipotent—that arm on which the pillars of the Heavens do lean. "Whom should I fear? The Lord is my strength and my life; of whom shall I be afraid?"

And this, may by grace, nerve you to work for God. If you had to save your neighbors you might sit down and do nothing; but since "salvation is of the Lord," go on and prosper. Go and preach the gospel; go and tell the Gospel everywhere. Tell it in your house, tell it in the street, tell it in every land and every nation; for it is not of yourself, it is "of the Lord." Why do not our friends go to Ireland to preach the Gospel? Ireland is a disgrace to the Protestant church. Why do not they go and preach there?

A year or so ago a number of our brave ministers went over there to preach; they did right bravely; they went there, and they came back again, and that is about the sum total of the glorious expedition against Catholicism. But why come back again? Because they were stoned, good easy men! Do they not think that the Gospel ever will spread without a few stones? But they would have been killed! Brave martyrs they! Let them be enrolled in the red chronicle. Did the martyrs of old, did the Apostles shrink from going to any country because they would have been killed? No, they were ready to die: and if half a dozen ministers had been killed in Ireland, it would have been the finest thing in the world for liberty in future; for after that the people dare not have touched us; the strong arm of the law would have put them down; we might have gone through every village of Ireland afterwards, and been at peace; the constabulary would soon have put an end to such infamous murder; it would have awakened the Protestantism of England to claim the liberty which is our right there as we give it elsewhere.

We shall never see any great change till we have some men in our ranks who are willing to be martyrs. That deep ditch can never be crossed till the bodies of a few of us shall fill it up; and after that it will be easy work to preach the Gospel there. Our brethren should go there once more. They can leave their white cravats at home, and the white feather too, and go forth with a brave heart and a bold spirit; and if the people mock and scoff, let them mock and scoff on. George Whitefield said, when he preached on Kennington Common, where they threw dead cats and rotten eggs at him, "This is only the manure of Methodism, the best thing in the world to make it grow; throw away as fast as you please."

And when a stone cut him on the forehead, he seemed to preach the better for a little blood-letting. Oh! For such a man to dare the mob, and then the mob would not need to be dared. Let us go there, recollecting that "salvation is of the Lord," and let us in every place and at every time preach God's Word, believing that God's Word is more than a match for man's sin, and God will yet be master over all the earth.

My voice fails me again, and my thoughts too, I was weary this morning, when I came into this pulpit, and I am weary now. Sometimes I am joyous and glad, and feel in the pulpit as if I could preach forever; at other times I feel glad to close; but yet with such a text I would that I could have finished up with all the might that mortal lip could summon. Oh! To let men know this, that their salvation is of God! Swearer, swear not against Him in whose hand thy breath is! Despiser, despise not Him who can save you or destroy you. And thou hypocrite, seek not to deceive Him from whom salvation comes, and who therefore knows right well whether thy salvation come from Him.

OBSERVANCE OF THIS TRUTH

And now in concluding, let me just tell you *what is the witness of this truth*. Salvation is of God: then damnation is of man. If any of you are damned, you will have no one to blame but yourselves; if any of you perish, the blame will not lie at God's door; if you are lost and cast away, you will have to bear all the blame and all the tortures of conscience yourself; you will lie forever in perdition, and reflect, "I have destroyed myself; I have made a suicide of my soul; I have been my own destroyer; I can lay no blame to God."

Remember, if saved, you must be saved by God alone, though if lost you have lost yourselves. "Turn ye, turn ye, why will ye die, O house of Israel." With my last faltering sentence I bid you stop and think. Ah! My hearers, my hearers! It is an awful thing to preach to such a mass as this. But the other Sunday, as I came down stairs, I was struck with a memorable sentence, uttered by one who stood there. He said, "There are 9,000 people this morning without excuse in the day of judgment." I should like to preach so that this always might be said; and if I cannot, oh may God have mercy on me, for his name's sake! But now remember! Ye have souls; those souls will be damned, or saved. Which will it be? Damned they must be forever, unless God shall save you; unless Christ shall have mercy upon you, there is no hope for you. Down on your knees. I Cry to God for mercy. Now lift up your heart in prayer to God. May now be the very time when you shall be saved. Or ever the next drop of blood shall run through your veins, may you find peace! Remember, that peace is to be had now. If you feel now your need of it, it is to be had now. And how? For the mere asking for it. "Ask, and it shall be given you; seek, and ye shall find."

> "But if your ears refuse
>   The language of his grace,
> Your hearts grow hard, like stubborn Jews,
>   That unbelieving race.
>
> "The Lord with vengeance drest,
>   Shall lift his hand and swear,

You that despised my promised rest
    Shall have no portion there."

Oh! That ye may not be despisers, lest ye "wonder and perish!" May ye now fly to Christ, and be accepted in the beloved. It is my last best prayer. May the Lord hear it. Amen.

2

Salvation All of Grace[1]

"By Grace are you saved" (Ephesians 2:8).

OTHER DIVINE ATTRIBUTES are manifest in Salvation. The Wisdom of God devised the plan; the Omnipotence of God executes in us the work of Salvation; the Immutability of God preserves and carries it on—in fact, all the Attributes of God are magnified in the Salvation of a sinner: but at the same time the text is most accurate, since Grace is the fountainhead of Salvation, and is most conspicuous throughout. Grace is to be seen in our Election, for, "There is a remnant according to the election of Grace, and if by Grace then it is no more of works." Grace is manifestly revealed in our Redemption, for you know therein the Grace of our Lord Jesus Christ, and it is utterly inconceivable that any soul could have deserved to be redeemed with the precious blood of Christ.

The mere thought is abhorrent to every holy mind. Our calling is also of Grace, too, for, "He has saved us, and called us with a holy calling, not according to our works, but according to His own purpose and

---

[1] A sermon delivered by C. H. Spurgeon on August 4, 1872 at the Metropolitan Tabernacle, Newington.

Grace, which was given us in Christ Jesus before the world began." By Grace also are we justified; for over and over again the Apostle insists upon this grand and fundamental Truth of God. We are not justified (declared *righteous*) before God by works in any measure or in any degree, but by faith alone; and the Apostle tells us, "It is of faith, that it might be by Grace." We see a golden thread of Grace running through the whole of the Christian's history, from his Election before all worlds, even to his admission to the Heaven of rest. Grace, all along, "Reigns through righteousness unto eternal life," and, "Where sin abounds, Grace does much more abound."

There is no point in the history of a saved soul upon which you can put your finger and say, "In this instance he is saved by his own merit." Every single blessing which we receive from God comes to us by the channel of free favor, revealed to us in Christ Jesus our Lord. Boasting is excluded because merits are excluded. Merit is an unknown word in the Christian Church; it is banished once and for all; and our only shouts over foundation or top stone are, "Grace, Grace unto it!"

Perhaps the Apostle is the more earnest in insisting upon this Truth of God here, and in many other places, because this is a point against which the human heart raises the greatest objection. Every man by nature fights against Salvation by Grace. Though we have nothing good in ourselves, we all think we have; though we have all broken the Law, and have lost all claim upon Divine Righteousness, yet we are all proud enough to fancy that we are not *quite as bad* as others; that there are some mitigating circumstances in our offenses, and that we can, in some measure, appeal to the Justice as well as to the Compassion of God. Hence the Apostle puts it so strongly, "By Grace are you saved, through faith, and that not of yourselves, it is the gift of God; not of works, lest any man should boast."

The statement of the Text means just this that we all need saving—saving from our sins, and saving from the consequences of them; and that if we are saved, it is not because of any works which we have already performed. Who among us, upon looking back at his past life, would dare to say that he deserves Salvation? Neither are we saved on account of any works foreseen which are yet to be performed by us; we have made no bargain with God that we will give Him so much service for so much mercy—neither has He made any Covenant with us of this character; He has freely saved us, and if we serve Him in the future, as we trust we shall, with all our heart, and soul, and strength, even then we shall have no room for glorying because our works are worked in us of the Lord!

What have we, then, which we have not received? We are saved not because of any mitigating circumstances with regard to our transgressions, nor because we were excusable on account of our youth, or of our ignorance, or any other cause; we are not saved because there were some good points in our character which ought not to be overlooked, or some hopeful indications of better things in the future! Ah, no—"By Grace are you saved;" that clear and unqualified statement sweeps away all supposition of any deserving on our part, or any thought of deserving! It is not a case of a prisoner at the bar who pleads, "Not guilty," and who escapes because he is innocent. Far from it, for we are guilty beyond all question!

It is not even a case of a prisoner who pleads, "Guilty," but at the same time mentions certain circumstances which render his offense less heinous. Far from it, for our offense is heinous to the last degree, and our sin deserves the utmost Wrath of God! Ours is the case of a criminal confessing his guilt, and acknowledging that he deserves the punishment, offering no extenuation, and making no apology, but casting himself upon the absolute mercy of the judge, desiring him, for pity's sake, to look upon his misery and spare him in compassion!

As condemned criminals, we stand before God when we come to Him for His Mercy; we are not in a state of probation, as some say; our probation is over—we are already lost! "Condemned already" and our only course is to cast ourselves upon the Sovereign Mercy of God in Christ Jesus, not uttering a syllable of claim, but simply saying, "Mercy, Lord, I crave undeserved Mercy according to Your Loving Kindness, and Your Grace in Christ Jesus." Because, "By Grace are you saved." This is true of every saint on earth and every saint in Heaven—altogether true without a single sentence of qualification! No man is saved *except as* the result of the free favor, and unbought Mercy of God; not of merit, not of debt; but entirely and altogether because the Lord "will have mercy on whom He will have mercy," and He wills to bestow His favor on the unworthy sons of men!

THE HOPE OF EVERY SINNER

This simple Truth of God we do not mean to work out this morning, doctrinally or controversially, but to use it for practical purposes, and the first is this—*this great doctrine should inspire every sinner with hope.* If Salvation is altogether of the free favor and Grace of God, then who among us dares to despair? Who in this place shall be so wicked as to sit down in sullenness and say, "It is impossible for me to be saved?"

For first, my Brothers and Sisters, if Salvation is of God's Mercy only, it is clear that our sin is by no means an impediment to our Salvation. If it were of justice, our transgression of the Law would render our Salvation utterly impossible; but if the Lord deals with us upon quite another footing, and says, "I will forgive them freely," that very Promise presupposes sin! If the Lord speaks of His Mercy, that very word takes it for granted that we are guilty, or else there would be no room for His

Mercy at all; the very statement that we are saved by Grace implies that we are fit objects for Grace, and who are fit objects for Grace but the guilty, the wretched, the condemned? Oh souls of men, the Law stops your mouths, and makes you silently admit that you are guilty before God; but the Gospel opens the mouth of the dumb by declaring, "Christ died for the ungodly," and, "He came into the world to save sinners." If Mercy comes into the field, sin is swallowed up in forgiveness, and unworthiness ceases to be a barrier for love! Is not this both clear and comforting?

Now observe that this prevents the despair which might arise in any heart on account of some one special sin. I meet with many whose terror of conscience arises from one particular crime; had they not committed that crimson sin, they consider that they might have been pardoned, but now they are in an evil case. "Surely," they say, "that sin, like an iron bolt, has fast closed the gates of Heaven against me."

And yet it cannot be so if Salvation is of Grace! Whatever the sin may be, its greatness will only serve to illustrate the great Grace of God. Undeserved Mercy can pardon one sin as well as another if the soul confesses it. If God acted on the rule of merit with us, then no sin would be pardonable under any circumstances, but when He deals with us in a way of Grace, He can pass by any offense for which we seek forgiveness. The great sinner is so much the fitter object for great Mercy; he who has but little sin, can, as it were, but draw forth little Mercy from God to blot it out; but he who is guilty of some great, crowning, damning sin—he it is to whom the heights and depths of Divine Mercy may be displayed!

And if I speak to such a one this morning, I would look upon him with joyful eyes; sorrowful as he is, I am thankful to have found out such a one; you are a rare platform on which my Lord's Love may display itself because you know yourself to be so utterly a lost sinner! You are but a black foil to set forth the brilliant diamond of my Master's Grace! Your foulness shall but illustrate the virtue of His precious blood; and your crimson sin, by yielding in a moment to the precious blood, shall only show how great His power to save is!

It is clear, too, that if the sinner's despair should arise from the long continuance, multitude, and great aggravation of his sins, there is no ground for it. For if Salvation is of pure Mercy only, why should not God forgive 10,000 sins as well as one?

"Oh," you say, "I see why He should not."

Then you see more than is true, for once come to Grace, you have done with bounds and limits! Know, moreover, that, "His thoughts are not your thoughts, and as the heavens are higher than the earth, so are His thoughts higher than your thoughts, and His ways than your ways." To blot out 10,000 sins is, with Him, no effort of Grace, for, "He is plenteous in Mercy." He has been forgiving the sons of men ever since the first sinner crossed the threshold of Paradise, and He delights to do it! So that, guilty Ones, I see in the multitude of your sins only so much the more room for the Lord to exercise His own delightful Attribute of Mercy! If He delights to blot out one sin, then He delights 10,000 times more to blot out 10,000 sins! If you will look at it in that light, though your transgressions may be as many as the hairs on your head, or as the sands on the seashore, you need not for a moment think you are cast away from hope! The Lord's Mercy is a sea which cannot be filled, though mountains of sin are cast into its midst! It is like Noah's flood which covers all, and drowns even the mountaintops of heaven-defying sins! I wish to speak right home to the hearts of those who are in trouble, and seeking God's Mercy, and to them I say—do you not see that if Salvation is of Grace alone, then the depravity of your nature does not shut you up in despair?

Though your Nature is inclined to sin, and especially inclined to some sins—what if you are naturally angry and passionate? What if you are proud and covetous? What if you are in your natural disposition skeptical or lustful? Yet from the Grace of God hope flows even for you! If the Lord were to deal with you according to your constitution and nature, then indeed it were a hopeless case with you; but if He blesses you, not because you are good, but because you need to be blessed; if He looks upon you in His Mercy, not because you are beautiful, but because you are sick unto death, and defiled, and need to be healed and cleansed; if it is your misery and not your merit which He considers, then you are yet in the land of hope! However fallen you may be, you may yet be raised up! Why should not the Lord take the most depraved and abandoned, and obstinate among us, and renew his nature, and make of him a miracle of Grace? Would it not magnify His Mercy if He should make of such a one the opposite of what he now is? What if He should make him tender in heart, Holy in spirit, devout in character, ardent in love, and fervent in prayer? He can do it! Glory be to His name; He can do it! And now that He deals with us in Grace, let us hope He will do it in the case of many here today.

Remember, too, that any spiritual unfitness which may exist in a man should not shut him out from a hope, since God deals with us in Mercy. I hear you say, "I believe God can save me, but I am so impenitent." Yes, and I say it again, if you were to stand on terms of debt with God, your hard heart would shut you out of hope; how could He bless such a wretch as you are, whose heart is a heart of stone? But if He deals with you entirely upon another ground, namely, His Mercy, why I think I hear Him say, "Poor hard-hearted Sinner, I will pity you, and take away your heart of stone, and give you a heart of flesh."

Do you say, "I cannot repent"? I know the criminality of that sad fact; it is a great sin not to be able to repent, but then the Lord will not look upon you from the point of what you ought to be, but He will consider what He can make you, and He will give you repentance! Has not His Son gone up to Heaven, "exalted on high, to give repentance and remission of sins?" Do I hear you confess that you cannot believe?

Now, the absence of faith from you is a great evil; yes, a horrible evil, but then the Lord is dealing with you on terms of Grace, and does not say, "I will not strike you because you do not believe," but He says, "I will give you faith," for faith is "not of yourselves, it is the gift of God." He works our faith in us, and has pity upon us, and takes away the unbelieving heart, and gives the tender heart, the believing heart, in the presence of the Cross of Christ! Oh, though I was black as the devil with past sin, and vile as the devil with innate depravity, yet, if the Lord's Mercy looked upon me, could He not forgive the past, and change my nature, and make me as bright a seraph as Gabriel before His Throne? "Is anything too hard for the Lord?" O Sinner, what a door of hope there ought to be open to you in this Truth of God—that Salvation is altogether of Grace!

And now, to sum up all in a word, there is no supposable circumstance or incident, or anything connected with any man or woman that can shut them out of hope if he seeks forgiveness through the Savior's blood! Whoever you may be, and whatever you may have done, Grace can come and save you!

I say again, if your character is the question at issue, you are lost! If your power to amend your character is the hinge of the business, you are lost! But if the Grace that pardons, and the power that amends both come from God, why should you be lost? Why should the harlot perish? Why should the thief perish? Why should the adulterer perish? Why should the murderer perish? "Let the wicked forsake his way, and the unrighteous man his thoughts, and let him turn unto the Lord, and He will have mercy upon him, and to our God, for He will abundantly pardon." You have heaped up your sins, but God will heap up His Mercy! You have highly aggravated your transgressions; you have sinned against light and knowledge; you have done evil with both hands greedily! But, thus says the Lord, "I have blotted out, as a thick cloud, your transgressions, and, as a cloud, your sins: return unto Me; for I have Redeemed you." So, "Come now, and let us reason together, says the Lord: though your sins are as scarlet, they shall be white as snow; though they are red like crimson, they shall be as wool."

DIRECTION TO SINNERS

Secondly, *this doctrine affords direction to the sinner* as to how to act before his God in seeking His Mercy. Clearly, O Soul, if Salvation is of Grace alone, it would be a very wrong course of action to plead that you are not guilty, or to extenuate your faults before God—that were to go upon the wrong tack altogether! If Salvation is by your merit, or by an absence of demerit, then you would be right enough to set up a good character as a plea, though I believe that in the trial you would break down mightily, for you are as full of sin as an egg is of meat, and your sin is as damnable as Hell itself! And, therefore, it would be vain for you to plead innocence—but if you could plead it, it is the wrong plea. If Salvation is of Grace, then go to the Lord, and confess your sin and transgression, and ask for Grace; do not for a moment attempt to show that you have no need of Grace, for that was folly indeed! What more foolish than for a beggar to plead that he is not in need? Do not shut the door of Grace in your own face! To say, "I am not guilty," is to say, "I do not need God's Mercy;" to say, "I have not transgressed," is to say, "I do not need to be forgiven," and how better could you commit spiritual suicide than by such pleading?

Neither, O Sinner, hope to propitiate the Lord with gifts and sacrifices. If Salvation is of Grace, how dare you think to buy it? If He says He gives it freely, bring not with you any bribe, for in so doing you will insult and anger Him. Indeed, what could you bring to Him when Lebanon is not sufficient to burn, nor the beasts thereof for a burnt sacrifice? If you could give Him rivers of oil that would deluge a continent, or seas of sacrificial blood broad as the Pacific, yet could you not for a moment render yourself acceptable with Him; therefore do not try it! Venture on no ceremonies; rest not in rituals; if Salvation is of Grace, accept it as a free gift, and bless the Giver. Do not think to dress yourself in garments of outward religiousness, or to borrow virtue from a fellow man who claims to be a priest; but since Salvation is of free Mercy, go and cast yourself on that free Mercy; that is to act according to the dictates of prudence. Your true course is this—since God is willing to show His Mercy, go and confess that you need His Mercy.

Aggravate your sin in the confession if you can; instead of trying to make it appear white, try to see its unutterable blackness; say that you are without excuse, justly condemned for your transgressions; I assure you, you shall never go beyond the truth in stating your sin, for that were quite impossible. A man lying wounded on the field of battle—when the surgeon comes round, or the soldiers with the ambulance, does not say, "Oh, mine is a little wound," for he knows that then they would let him lie. But he cries out, "I have been bleeding here for hours, and am nearly dead with a terrible wound," for he thinks that then he will gain speedier relief; and when he gets into the hospital, he does not say to the nurse, "Mine is a small affair; I shall soon get over it," but he tells the truth to the surgeon in the hope that he may set the bone at once, and that double care may be taken.

Ah, Sinner, you must do the same with God! The right way to plead is to plead your misery, your impotence, your danger, your sin! Lay bare your wounds before the Lord, and as Hezekiah spread Sennacherib's letter before the Lord, spread your sins before Him with many a tear, and many a cry, and say, "Lord, save me from all these; save me from these black and foul things for Your Infinite Mercy's sake." Confess your sin! Wisdom dictates that you should do so, since Salvation is of Grace. And then yield yourself up to God; make no terms with Him, but say,

> "Here I stand before You, O my Maker; I have offended You; I yield to You because You have said You will deal with me on terms of Grace. Behold, I cast myself at Your feet; the weapons of my rebellion I cast from my hands forever! I desire that You would take me, and make me what You would have me to be; and seeing You are a God of Grace, I beseech You to have pity upon me. You have appointed a way of Salvation by Jesus Christ; oh, save me in that way, I entreat You."

Now, I need to dwell upon this next point: because Salvation is of Grace, it directs the guilty as to how to plead before God. When we are praying and pleading, we sometimes feel we need a help to guide us in the pleading. Let this guide you: take care that all your pleas with God are consistent with the fact that He saves by His Grace. Never bring a legal plea, or a plea that is based upon self, for it will be an offense to God; whereas, if your argument is based on Grace, it will have a sweet savor to Him. Let me teach you, seeking Sinner, for a moment how to pray. Let it be in this way. Plead with God your miserable and undone condition; tell Him you are utterly lost if He does not save you; tell Him you are already lost, so that you cannot help yourself hand or foot in this matter if He does not come to your rescue with the fullness of His Power and Love. Tell him that you are afraid to die, and to come before His righteous bar, for unless He saves you, Hell will be your portion. Plead with Him, and ask Him whether it will delight Him that you should make your bed in Hell. Say to Him, "Shall the dead praise You? Shall the condemned set forth Your praise?" Show Him the imminence of your danger; He knows it, but let Him see that you know it! This will be good pleading with His

Mercy: "Save me, O Lord, for if ever a soul needed saving, if ever a soul was in the jaws of destruction, I am that soul! Therefore have pity upon me."

Thus pour out your heart before Him. Then humbly urge the suitableness of His Mercy to you:

"Lord, You are Merciful; Your Mercy will find ample scope in me. Does your Grace seek out sin to purge it away? It is here, Lord! I teem with it—my heart swarms with evils! If You are Merciful, here is a heart which bleeds, and is ready to perish. Oh, if You are, indeed, a Physician, here is a sick soul that needs You! If You are ready to forgive, here are sins that need forgiving; come to me, Lord, for Your Mercy will find a grievousness of misery in me! Besides, is not Your Mercy free? It is true I do not deserve it, but You do not give it to men because of their merit, else were it not Grace and Mercy at all!

Let Your free Mercy light on me! Why should You pass me by? If I am the vilest of the sons of men, You will be the more gracious if You look upon me! Though I have forgotten You these many years, and have even despised Your Love, will it not be the greater Mercy on Your part to turn and give Your free Grace to me, even to me?"

Then argue with Him the plenteousness of His Grace. Say to Him,

"Lord, Your Mercy is very great; I know it is. 'According to the multitude of Your tender Mercies, blot out my transgressions.' If You were a little God, and You had but little Mercy, I should have but little hope in You, but oh, You are so great and glorious; You can cast my transgressions behind Your back; by the greatness of Your Compassion, look on me."

It is also well to return to the first plea, and repeat it, saying,

"Lord, because You have this great Mercy, and I need it, look on my impotence this day. I am so weak I cannot come to You, unless You come to me. You bid me repent, but see how hard my heart is! You command me to believe in Jesus, but my unbelief is very strong! You tell me to look to Your dear Son upon the Cross, but I cannot see Him for my tears which blind these weary eyes. Master, come to the rescue! Come and help Your servant, for You are strong, and I am weak. You can break my heart though I cannot break it, and You can open my poor bleared eyes, though I cannot as yet see as I would see the Savior Jesus Christ. Oh, by Your Power and Mercy, save a weak, dead sinner."

And then, if you feel as if you needed some other plea, begin to plead His Promises. Say—

> "You have promised to forgive
> All who on Your Son believe.
> Lord, I know You cannot lie;
> Give me Christ or else I die!

"You have said that if the wicked forsake his way and turn unto You, he shall live. Lord, I turn to You! Receive me! You have said that all manners of sin and of blasphemy shall be forgiven unto men. You have declared that the blood of Jesus Christ Your Son cleanses from all sin. Go not back from Your Word, O God! Since You are dealing with men on terms of Grace, keep Your Promise, and let Your rich, free Mercy come to me."

I know what all this means by experience; I have gone over all these pleas by the week together, and pleaded with God that He would have Mercy upon me. "This poor man cried, and the Lord heard him, and delivered him from all his fears." Therefore, I bear testimony unto you, O seeking Souls, that this is the way to move His heart; go upon the plan of Grace and plead His Love. Never plead your merits, but your demerits! Never your profession of what you hope to do, but your acknowledgment of your misery will have power with Him.

I have found it sweet work, sometimes, to plead with God His Mercy in the gifts of Christ. Let me help you, Sinner, to do it, and may the Spirit help you. Say unto God thus,

> "Lord, You have given Your Only-Begotten Son to die. Surely He need not have died for the righteous; He died for the guilty. I am such a one—Lord, will You give Your Son for sinners, and then cast sinners away? Did You nail Him to the Cross only for a mockery, that we might come to that Cross and not find pity? O God of Mercy, in the gift of Your Son You have done so much that You cannot draw back! You must save sinners now that You have given Jesus to die for them."

Then plead with Jesus the compassion of His heart; tell Him that He said He would not break the bruised reed, nor quench the smoking flax. Pluck Him by the sleeve, and say, "You have said, 'Him that comes unto Me, I will in no wise cast out.'" Tell Him that it was written of Him, "This Man receives sinners, and eats with them." Tell Him that you have heard, "This is a faithful saying, and worthy of all acceptation, that Christ Jesus came into the world to save sinners;" and say to Him, "Have You lost your Compassion, Savior? Will You not dart a glance of Love on me, even me? You healed lepers—heal my leprosy! You permitted the woman You called a dog, to come and receive blessings at Your hands, and although I am a dog, yet give the crumbs of Your Mercy to me, even me." This is the style of plea that will win the day.

And then I would advise you, if you still fail in prayer, to go to God, and say to Him, "Lord, You have sworn with an oath—'As I live, says the

Lord, I have no pleasure in the death of him that dies, but had rather that he would turn to Me and live.' I know that you mean this, my God. Will You take pleasure, then, in my death, and spurn me now that I turn to You?"

Tell Him that He has saved other sinners like you; remind Him of your wife, or child, or friend; tell Him of Saul of Tarsus; tell Him of the woman who was a sinner. Tell Him of Rahab, and say unto Him, "Lord, do You not delight to save great, big, evil sinners? I am just such a one! You have not changed; by all that You have done for others, I pray You do the same for me." And then say to Him again,

> "I thank You, O God, that You have permitted even me to pray to You; I bless Your Grace that You have moved me to come to You; and as You have given me Grace to feel my sin in a measure, will You leave me to perish after all? Oh, by the Grace I have received in being spared so long in being permitted to hear Your Gospel, I beseech You to give me more Grace!"

Then throw yourself down before Him, and if you perish, perish there! Go to the Cross with such pleas as these, and resolve that if it can be that a sinner may die at the foot of the Cross, you will die there, but nowhere else! As the Lord my God lives, before whom I stand, there shall never a soul perish that can cast itself upon the Sovereign Grace of God through Jesus Christ His Son!

CONVICTION LEADS TO RECONCILIATION

Now, to turn away from that to a third point. *A full conviction of this truth will reconcile our hearts to all divine ordinances with regard to salvation.* I feel in my own heart, and I think every Believer here does, that if Salvation is of Grace, God must do as He wills with His own. None of us can say to Him, "What are You doing?" If there were anything of debt, or justice, or obligation in the matter, then we might begin to question God—but as there is none, and the thing is quite out of court as to law, and far away from rights and claims, as it is all God's free favor, we will, therefore, stop our mouths, and never question Him. As to the persons whom He chooses to save, let Him save whom He wills; His name shall be had in honor forever, let His choice be what it may; as to the instrument by which He saves, let Him save by the coarsest speaker, or by the most eloquent; let Him do what seems good to Him. If He will save by the Bible, without ministers, we will be glad to hold our tongues! And if He will save souls by one of our Brothers, and not by us, we will grieve to think that we are so little fitted for His service, but still, if after doing all we can, He uses another more than us, we will say, "Blessed be His name." We will not envy our Brothers; the Lord shall distribute His Grace by what hands He pleases. Send, Lord, by whomever You will send!

And here I come to the sinner again: with the two great Gospel commands we will raise no dispute. Has He said, "He that believes, and is baptized shall be saved?" We will never raise a question against either the believing or the Baptism! If the Lord chooses to say, "I will save those who trust in Christ," it is both so natural a thing that He should claim our faith, and so gracious a thing that He should give us the faith He claims of us, that we cannot question it! And even if it were not so, He has a right to make what rules He pleases; if God permits entrance only by one door, let us enter by it, and raise no contention. The Lord bids you trust in Jesus—say not in your heart, "I would rather do or feel some wonderful matter." If He had bid you do some great thing, would you not have done it? How much rather, now, that He says to you, simply trust in Jesus and be saved? I know if I were authorized to preach this morning that every man who would sail round the world should be saved, you would begin saving your money to make the great excursion!

But when the Gospel comes to you there in those very pews and aisles, and bids you now turn your eyes to the Crucified Savior, and only look to Him, I know if you have not learned the Truth of God, that Salvation is of Grace, you will kick at that Divine Command! But if you know it is of Grace, and only Grace, you will say, "Sweet is the Command of God! Lord, enable me, now, to trust myself with Your dear Son."

And then, you will not quarrel with the Ordinance of Baptism, either. I know it is very natural that you should say, "What is there in it?" I also would say, what is there in it? What can there be in a mere washing in water? If you thought there were any Salvation by it meritoriously, you would have missed the track altogether! But the Lord has put it, that "he who believes, and is baptized, shall be saved," and therefore you must obey! I do not attempt to justify my Lord for so commanding, for He needs no defense from me; but if He so chooses to put it, the true heart will yield a prompt obedience to His will. If it were of merit, I could see no merit in Baptism or in the believing, for surely it cannot be meritorious to believe what is true, or to have one's body washed with pure water. But Salvation is of Grace—and if the Lord chooses to put it so, let Him put it as He wills! I am such a sinner, I will take His Mercy, let Him present it in what way He pleases.

As to the manner in which the Lord may be pleased to reveal Himself to any one of us, I am sure that if we know that Salvation is of Grace, we shall never quarrel about that any more. To some of us, the Lord revealed Himself on a sudden; we know when we were converted to the day! I know the place to a yard, but many others do not. The day breaks on them gradually—first twilight, and then a brighter light—and afterwards comes the noon. Do not let us quarrel about that. So long as I get a Savior, I do not mind how I get Him! So long as He blots out my sins, I will not quibble about the way in which He manifests His Love to me. If it is of Grace, that silences everything—Jew and Gentile shut their mouths without a murmuring word—and all together sit down at the foot of the Cross, no more to question, but reverently to adore!

THE MOTIVE FOR HOLINESS

I pass over this point rapidly, for time flies. I gladly would clip his wings. But I must introduce to you the next fact—that the doctrine that Salvation is of Grace furnishes to those who receive it *a most powerful motive for future holiness.*

A man who feels that he is saved by Grace says, "Did God of His free favor blot out my sins? Then, oh, how I love Him! Was it nothing but His Love that saved an undeserving wretch? Then my soul is knit to Him forever." Great sin becomes in such a case no barrier to great Holiness, but rather a motive for it, for he who has had much forgiven, loves much, and loving much, he begins at once to be in earnest in the service of Him whom he loves! I put it to you, Sinner, if the Lord this morning were to appear to you and say, "All your sins have been blotted out," would you not love Him? Yes, I think a dog would love such a Master as that! Would you not love Him? Yes, I know you would!

I know you proud, self-righteous people would not—but you real sinners, if pardon were to come to you—would you not love God with all your hearts? Assuredly you would, and then your soul would begin to burn with a desire to honor Him! You would need to tell the next person you met—"The Lord has had Mercy upon me! Wonder of wonders, He has had Mercy upon me!" And then you would desire to put away everything that would displease Him. Away, you Sins! Away, you Sins; how can I defile myself with you again? And then you would desire to practice all His will, and say, "For the love I bear His name, no duty shall be too difficult, no command too severe."

There are none who love God like those who are saved by Grace! The man who thinks to save himself by works does not love God at all; he loves himself—he is a servant working for wages, and that is the kind of servant who would turn to another master tomorrow if he could get better paid! And if the wages do not suit him, he will strike. The old-fashioned servants were the best servants in the world, for they loved their masters, and if paid no wages at all would have stuck to the family for love's sake. Such are the servants of God who are saved by His Grace. "Why," they say, "He has already pardoned me, and saved me, and therefore my ear is bored, and fastened to the door of His house to be His servant forever; and my glory is, 'I am Your servant, I am Your servant, and the son of Your handmaid, You have loosed my bonds.'" Such a man feels that he must perfect Holiness in the fear of the Lord. He will not stop short with a measure of Grace—he wants immeasurable Grace!

He will not say, "There are some sins in me which I cannot overcome," but by God's Grace he will seek to drive out all the Amalekites! He will not say, "Up to this point I am commanded to go, but beyond that I have a license to say, 'That is my besetting sin; I cannot get rid of it.'" No, but loving God with all his heart, he will hate sin with all his heart, and war with sin with all his might, and will never put sword in scabbard till he is perfected in the Image of Christ! The Lord fires us with such ardent love as this, and I know no way by which to get it except by coming to Him on terms of Grace, confessing sin, receiving His Mercy, feeling His Love kindled in the heart in consequence, and thus the whole soul becomes consecrated to the Lord.

A TEST FROM THE TEXT

Lastly, I wish I could handle my text as I desire, and as it handles me, but the truth of my text will be *a test for this congregation*. The way you treat this text shall well reveal what you are. It will be either a stone of stumbling to you this morning, or else a foundation stone on which you build. Is it a stone of stumbling? Did I hear you murmur, "Why, the man does not hold up morality and good works; he preaches Salvation for the guilty and the vile; I do not need such a religion!"?

Alas, you have stumbled at this stumbling stone, and shall be broken upon it. You shall perish, for you do insult your God by thinking yourself wiser than His Word, and by fancying that your righteousness is purer than the Righteousness of Christ! You imagine you can force your way to Heaven by a road that is most effectually blocked up! You despise the path which the Lord has opened! Beware of self-righteousness! The black devil of licentiousness destroys his hundreds, but the white devil of self-righteousness destroys his thousands!

But do you accept this text as a foundation stone? Do you say, "I need Grace, indeed, for I am guilty?" Then come and take all the blessings of the Covenant, for they are yours! "He has put down the mighty from their seat, and He has exalted them of low degree; He has filled the hungry with good things, but the rich He has sent away empty." Are you guilty? Come and trust your Savior! Are you empty? Come and be filled out of the fullness which is treasured up in Christ Jesus! Believe in Jesus now, for one act of faith sets you free from all sin! Do not tarry for a moment, nor raise questions with your God; believe Him capable of Infinite Mercy, and through Jesus Christ rest in Him. If you are the worst soul in the world in your own apprehension, and the one odd man that would be left out of every catalog of Grace, now write not such things against yourself—or even if you do, come and cast yourself upon your

God! He cannot reject you or if He should, you would be the first that ever trusted in Him and was refused!

Come and try! Oh, that His Spirit may bring you to Jesus at this very moment, and that in Heaven there may be joy in the presence of the angels of God because a soul has confided in the Grace of God, and found immediate pardon and instantaneous Salvation through the precious blood of Christ! The Lord bless every one of you!

Oh, how I would like that every soul here should be washed in the blood of Christ this morning! Would God that every one of you was robed in the Righteousness of Christ this day, and prepared to enter into His rest! Pray for it, Christian Brothers and Sisters! Why should we not have it? Why, this congregation, great as it may seem, comparatively, is very little to God! Why should there be one left out? Let your prayers encircle the whole house and bear the entire audience up to God! Lay it before Him and say, "By Your Mercy, and by Your Loving Kindness save all this gathered company, for Christ's sake." Amen.

3

Salvation Altogether By Grace[1]

"Who hath saved us, and called us with an holy calling, not according to our works, but according to his own purpose and grace which was given us in Christ Jesus before the world began" (2 Timothy 1:9).

I F WE WOULD INFLUENCE thoughtful persons it must be by solid arguments. Shallow minds may be wrought upon by mere warmth of emotion and force of excitement, but the more valuable part of the community must be dealt with in quite another manner. When the apostle Paul was desirous to influence his son in the faith, Timothy, who was a diligent and earnest student and a man of gifts as well as of grace, he did not attempt to affect him by mere appeals to his feelings, but felt that the most effectual way to act upon him was to remind him of solid doctrinal truth which he knew him to have believed.

This is a lesson for the ministry at large. Certain earnest preachers are incessantly exciting the people, and but seldom if ever instructing them; they carry much fire and very little light. God forbid that we

---

[1] A sermon delivered by C. H. Spurgeon on July 29, 1866 at the Metropolitan Tabernacle, Newington.

should say a word against appealing to the feelings; this is most needful in its place, but then there is a due proportion to be observed in it. A religion which is based upon, sustained, and maintained simply by excitement, will necessarily be very flimsy and unsubstantial, and will yield very speedily to the crush of opposition or to the crumbling hand of time.

The preacher may touch the feelings by rousing appeals, as the harper touches the harp strings; he will be very foolish if he should neglect so ready and admirable an instrument; but still as he is dealing with reasonable creatures, he must not forget to enlighten the intellect and instruct the understanding. And how can he appeal to the understanding better than by presenting to it the truth which the Holy Spirit teacheth? Scriptural doctrine must furnish us with powerful motives to urge upon the minds of Christians.

It seems to me that if we could by some unreasoning impulse move you to a certain course of action it might be well in its way, but it would be unsafe and untrustworthy, for you would be equally open to be moved in an opposite direction by other persons more skillful in such operations; but if God enables us by His Spirit to influence your minds by solid truth and substantial argument, you will then move with a constancy of power which nothing can turn aside.

The feather flies in the wind, but it has no inherent power to move, and consequently when the gale is over it falls to the ground—such is the religion of excitement; but the eagle has life within itself, and its wings bear it aloft and onward whether the breeze favors it or not—such is religion, when sustained by a conviction of the truth. The well-taught man in Christ Jesus stands firm where the uninstructed infant would fall or be carried away. "Be not carried about with every wind of doctrine," says the apostle, and those are least likely to be so carried who are well established in the truth as it is in Jesus.

It is somewhat remarkable—at least it may seem so to persons who are not accustomed to think upon the subject—that the apostle, in order to excite Timothy to boldness, to keep him constant in the faith, reminds him of the great doctrine that the grace of God reigns in the salvation of men. He gives in this verse—this parenthetical verse as some call it, but which seems to me to be fully in the current of the passage—he gives in this verse a brief summary of the gospel, showing the great prominence which it gives to the grace of God, with the design of maintaining Timothy in the boldness of his testimony for Christ.

I do not doubt but that a far greater power for usefulness lies concealed within the doctrines of grace than some men have ever dreamed of. It has been usual to look upon doctrinal truth as being nothing more than unpractical theory, and many have spoken of the precepts of God's Word as being more practical and more useful; the day may yet come when in clearer light we shall perceive that sound doctrine is the very root and vital energy of practical holiness, and that to teach the people the truth which God has revealed is the readiest and surest way of leading them to obedience and persevering holiness.

May the Holy Spirit assist us while we shall, first, consider the doctrine taught by the apostle in this text; and, secondly, the uses of that doctrine.

THE BIBLICAL TEXT UNDER CONSIDERATION

Very carefully, let us *consider the doctrine taught by the apostle in this text*.

Friends will remember that it is not our object to preach the doctrine which is most popular or most palatable, nor do we desire to set forth the views of any one person in the assembly; our aim is to give what we judge to be the meaning of the text. We shall probably deliver doctrine which many of you will not like, and if you should not like it we shall not be at all surprised, or even if you be vexed and angry we shall not be at all alarmed, because we never understood that we were commissioned to preach what would please our hearers, nor were expected by sensible, not to say gracious men, to shape our views to suit the notions of our audience. We count ourselves amenable to God and to the text; and if we give the meaning of the text, we believe we shall give the mind of God, and we shall be likely to have His favor, which will be sufficient for us, contradict us who may. However, let every candid mind be willing to receive the truth, if it be clearly in the inspired Word.

1. The apostle in stating his doctrine in the following words, "Who hath saved us, and called us with an holy calling, not according to our works, but according to his own purpose and grace, which was given us in Christ Jesus before the world began," declares God to be the author of salvation—"Who hath saved us and called us." The whole tenor of the verse is towards a strong affirmation of Jonah's doctrine, that "salvation is of the Lord." It would require very great twisting, involving more than ingenuity, it would need dishonesty, to make our salvation by man out of this text; but to find salvation altogether of God in it is to perceive the truth which lies upon the very surface. No need for profound inquiry, the wayfaring man though a fool shall not err therein; for the text says as plainly as words can say, "*God has* saved us, and called us with a holy calling."

The apostle, then, in order to bring forth the truth that salvation is of grace declares that it is of God, that it springs directly and entirely from Him and from Him only. Is not this according to the teaching of the Holy Spirit in other places, where He affirms over and over again that the alpha and omega of our salvation must be found, not in ourselves, but in our God?

Our apostle is saying that God hath saved us refers to all the persons of the Divine Unity. The Father hath saved us. "God hath given to us eternal life" (1 John 5:2). "The Father himself loveth you." It was He whose gracious mind first conceived the thought of redeeming His chosen from the ruin of the fall; it was His mind which first planned the way of salvation by substitution; it was from His generous heart that the thought first sprang that Christ should suffer as the covenant head of His people, as saith the apostle,

> "Blessed be the God and Father of our Lord Jesus Christ, who hath blessed us with all spiritual blessings in heavenly places in Christ. According as he hath chosen us in him before the foundation of the world, that we should be holy and without blame before him in love: having predestinated us unto the adoption of children by Jesus Christ to himself, according to the good pleasure of his will, to the praise of the glory of his grace, wherein he hath made us accepted in the Beloved" (Eph. 1:3-6).

From the bowels of divine compassion came the gift of the only begotten Son: "For God so loved the world, that he gave his only begotten Son, that whosoever believeth in him should not perish, but have everlasting life." The Father selected the persons who should receive an interest in the redemption of His Son, for these are described as "called according to his purpose" (Rom. 8:28). The plan of salvation in all its details sprang from the Father's wisdom and grace.

The apostle did not, however, overlook the work of the Son. It is most certainly through the Son of God that we are saved, for is not His name Jesus, the Savior? Incarnate in the flesh, His holy life is the righteousness in which saints are arrayed; while His ignominious and painful death has filled the sacred bath of blood in which the sinner must be washed that he may be made clean. It is through the redemption which is in Christ Jesus that the people of God become accepted in the Beloved. With one consent before the eternal throne they sing, "Unto him that loved us and washed us from our sin in his blood, unto him be glory;" and they chant that hymn because He deserves the glory which they ascribe to Him. It is the Son of God who is the Savior of men, and men are not the saviors of themselves.

Nor did the apostle, I am persuaded, forget that Third Person in the blessed Unity—the Holy Spirit. Who but the Holy Spirit first gives us power to understand the gospel? After all, "the carnal mind understandeth not the things that be of God." Does not the Holy Spirit influence our will, turning us from the obstinacy of our former rebellion to the obedience of the truth? Does not the Holy Spirit renew us, creating us in Christ Jesus unto good works? Is it not by the Holy Spirit's breath that we live in the spiritual life? Is He not to us Instructor, Comforter, Quickener; is He not *everything*, in fact, through His active operations upon our mind? The Father, then, in planning, the Son in redeeming, the Spirit in applying the redemption must be spoken of as the one God "who hath saved us."

Brethren, to say that we save ourselves is to utter a manifest absurdity. We are called in Scripture "a temple"—a holy temple in the Lord. But shall any one assert that the stones of the edifice were their own architect? Shall it be said that the stones of the building in which we are now assembled cut themselves into their present shape, and then spontaneously came together, and piled this spacious edifice? Should anyone assert such a foolish thing, we should be disposed to doubt his sanity; much more may we suspect the spiritual sanity of any man who should venture to affirm that the great temple of the church of God designed and erected itself. No; we believe that God the Father was the architect, sketched he plan, supplies the materials, and *will complete* the work.

Shall it also be said that those who are redeemed redeemed themselves? Or that slaves of Satan break their own fetters? Then why was a Redeemer needed at all? How should there be any need for Jesus to descend into the world to redeem those who could redeem themselves? Do you believe that the sheep of God, whom He has taken from between the jaws of the lion, could have rescued themselves? It was a strange thing indeed if such were the case.

Our Lord Jesus came not to do a work of supererogation, but if He came to save persons who might have saved themselves, He certainly came without a necessity for so doing. We cannot believe that Christ came to do what the sinners might have done themselves. No. "He hath trodden the winepress alone, and of the people there was none with him," and the redemption of His people shall give glory unto Himself only.

Shall it be asserted that those who were once dead have spiritually quickened themselves? Can the dead make themselves alive? Who shall assert that Lazarus, rotting in the grave, came forth to life of himself? If it be so said and so believed, then, nay, not even then, will we believe that the dead in sin have ever quickened themselves. Those who are saved by God the Holy Spirit are created afresh according to Scripture; but who ever dreamed of creation creating itself? God spoke the world out of nothing, but nothing did not aid in the creation of the universe. Divine energy can do everything, but what can *nothing* do? Now if we have a new creation, there must have been a creator, and it is clear that not being then spiritually created, we could not have assisted in our own new creation, unless, indeed, death can assist life, and non-existence aid in creation. The carnal mind does not assist the Spirit of God in new creating a man, but altogether regeneration is the work of God the Holy Spirit, and the work of renewal is from His unassisted power.

Father, Son, and Spirit we then adore, and putting these thoughts together, we would humbly prostrate ourselves at the foot of the throne of the august majesty, and acknowledge that if saved He alone hath saved us, and unto Him be the glory.

2. We next remark that grace is in this verse rendered conspicuous when we see that God pursues a singular method, "Who hath saved us and called us." The peculiarity of the manner lies in three things—first, in the completeness of it. The apostle uses the perfect tense and says, "who hath saved us." Believers in Christ Jesus are saved. They are not looked upon as persons who are in a hopeful state and may ultimately be saved, but they are *already* saved. This is not according to the common talk of professors now-a-days, for many of them speak of being saved when they come to die; but it is according to the usage of Scripture to speak of us who are saved. Be it known this morning that every man and woman here is either saved at this present moment or lost, and that salvation is not a blessing to be enjoyed upon the dying bed and to be sung of in a future state above, but a matter to be obtained, received, promised and enjoyed now. God hath saved His saints, mark, not partly saved them, but perfectly saved them.

The Christian is perfectly saved in God's purpose; God has ordained him unto salvation, and that purpose is complete. He is saved also as to the price which has been paid for him; for this is not in part but in whole. The substitutionary work which Christ has offered is not a certain proportion of the work to be done, but "it is finished" was the cry of the Savior before He died. The believer is also perfectly saved in his covenant head, for as we were utterly lost as soon as ever Adam fell, before we had committed any actual sin, so every man in Christ was saved in the second Adam when He finished His work. The Savior completed His work, and in the sense in which Paul uses that expression, "He hath saved us."

What?! Saved us before He called us? Yes, so the text says. But is a man saved before he is called by grace? Not in his own experience, not as far as the work of the Holy Spirit goes, but he is saved in God's purpose, in Christ's redemption, and in his relationship to his covenant Head; and he is saved, moreover, in this respect, that the work of his salvation is done, and he has only to receive it as a finished work.

In the olden times of imprisonment for debt, it would have been quite correct for you to step into the cell of a debtor and say to him, "I have freed you," if you had paid his debts and obtained an order for his discharge. Well, but he is still in prison. Yes; but you really liberated him as soon as you paid his debts. It is true he was still in prison, but he was not legally there, and no sooner did he know that the debt was paid, and that receipt was pleaded before proper authorities, than the man obtained his liberty. So the Lord Jesus Christ paid the debts of His people before they knew anything about it. Did He not pay them on the cross more than eighteen hundred years ago to the utmost penny? And is not this the reason why, as soon as He meets with us in a way of grace, He cries, "I have saved thee; lay hold on eternal life." We are, then, virtually, though not actually, saved before we are called. "He hath saved us and called us."

There is yet a third peculiarity, and that is in connection with the calling. God has called us with a holy calling. Those whom the Savior saved upon the tree are in due time effectually called by the power of God the Holy Spirit unto holiness; they leave their sins, they endeavor to be like Christ, they choose holiness, not out of any compulsion, but from the stress of a new nature, which leads them to rejoice in holiness, just as naturally as aforetime they delighted in sin. Whereas their old nature loved everything that was evil, their new nature cannot sin because it is born of God, and it loveth everything that is good. Does not the apostle mention this result of our calling in order to meet those who say that God calls His people because He foresees their holiness? Not so; He calls them to that holiness; that holiness is not a *cause* but an *effect*; it is not the motive of His purpose, but the result of His purpose. He neither chose them nor called them because they were holy, but He called them that they might be holy, and holiness is the beauty produced by His workmanship in them. The excellences which we see in a believer are as much the work of God as the atonement itself.

This second point brings out very sweetly the fullness of the grace of God. First: salvation must be of grace, because the Lord is the author of it; and what motive but grace could move Him to save the guilty? In the next place, salvation must be of grace, because the Lord works in such a manner that our righteousness is forever excluded. Salvation is completed by God, and therefore not of man, neither by man; salvation is wrought by God in an order which puts our holiness as a consequence and not as a cause, and therefore merit is forever disowned.

3. When a speaker desires to strengthen his point and to make himself clear, he generally puts in a negative as to the other side. So the apostle adds a negative: "Not according to our works." The world's great preaching is, "Do as well as you can, live a moral life, and God will save you." The Gospel preaching is this:

> "Thou art a lost sinner, and thou canst deserve nothing of God but His displeasure; if thou art to be saved, it must be by an act of sovereign grace. God must freely extend the silver sceptre of His love to thee, for thou art a guilty wretch who deserves to be sent to the lowest Hell. Thy best works are so full of sin that they can in no degree save thee; to the free mercy of God thou must owe all things."

"Oh," saith one, "are good works of no use?" God's works are of use when a man is saved, they are the evidences of his being saved; but good works do not save a man; good works do not influence the mind of God to save a man, for if so, salvation would be a matter of debt and not of grace. The Lord has declared over and over in His Word, "Not of works, lest any man should boast." And, "By the works of the law there shall no flesh living be justified."

The apostle in the epistle to the Galatians is very strong indeed upon this point; indeed he thunders it out again, and again, and again. He denies that salvation is even so much as in part due to our works, for if it be by work then he declares it is not of grace, otherwise grace is no more grace; and if it be of grace it is not of works, otherwise work is no more work. Paul assures us that the two principles of *grace* and *merit* can no more mix together than fire and water; that if man is to be saved by the mercy of God, it must be by the mercy of God and not by works; but if man is to be saved by works, it must be by works entirely and not by mercy mixed therewith, for mercy and work will not go together. Jesus saves, but He does all the work or none. He is Author and Finisher, and works must not rob Him of His due.

Sinner, you must either receive salvation freely from the hand of Divine Bounty, or else you must earn it by your own unassisted merits, which last is utterly impossible. Oh that you would yield to the first!

My brethren, this is the truth which still needs to be preached. This is the truth which shook all Europe from end to end when Luther first proclaimed it. Is not this the old thunderbolt which the great Reformer hurled at Rome—"Justified freely by his grace, through the redemption which is in Christ Jesus?" But why did God make salvation to be by faith? Scripture tells us—"therefore it is of faith, that it might be by grace." If it had been by works it must have been by debt; but since it is by faith, we can clearly see that there can be no merit in faith. It must be, therefore, by grace.

4. My text is even more explicit yet, for the eternal purpose is mentioned. The next thing the apostle says is this: "Who hath saved us, and called us with a holy calling, not according to our works but

according to his own purpose." Mark that phrase—"according to his own purpose."

Oh, how some people wriggle over that phrase, as if they were worms on a fisherman's hook! But there it stands, and cannot be got rid of. God saves His people "according to his purpose," nay, "according to his *own* purpose."

My brethren and sisters, do you not see how all merit and the power of the creature are shut out here, when you are saved, not according to your purpose or merit, but "according to his own purpose"? I shall not dwell on this; it is not exactly the object of this morning's discourse to bring out in full the great mystery of electing love, but I will not for a moment keep back the truth. If any man be saved, it is not because he purposed to be saved, but because God purposed to save him.

Have you never read the Holy Spirit's testimony: "It is not of him that willeth, nor of him that runneth, but of God that showeth mercy?" The Savior said to His apostles what He in effect says also to us, "Ye have not chosen me, but I have chosen you and ordained you, that ye might bring forth fruit." Some hold one and some another view concerning the freedom of the will, but our Savior's doctrine is, "Ye will not come unto me, that ye might have life." You will not come; your wills will never bring you; if you do come, it is because grace inclined you. "No man can come unto me, except the Father which hath sent me draw him." And, "Whosoever cometh to me I will in no wise cast out," is a great and precious general text, but it is quite consistent with the rest of the same verse—"All the Father giveth me *shall come* to me."

Our text tells us that our salvation is "according to his own purpose." It is a strange thing that men should be so angry against the purpose of God. We ourselves have a purpose; we permit our fellow creatures to have some will of their own, and especially in giving away their own goods; but my God is to be bound and fettered by men, and not permitted to do as He wills with His own. But be this known unto you, Oh men that reply against God, that He giveth no account of His matters, but asks of you, "Can I not do as I will with mine own?" He ruleth in Heaven, and in the armies of this lower world, and none can stay His hand or say unto Him, "What doest thou?"

5. But then the text, lest we should make any mistake, adds, "according to his own purpose and grace." The purpose is not founded on foreseen merit, but upon grace alone. It is grace, all grace, nothing but grace from first to last. Man stands shivering outside, a condemned criminal, and God sitting upon the throne, sends the herald to tell him that He is willing to receive sinners and to pardon them. The sinner replies, "Well, I am willing to be pardoned if I am permitted to do something in order to earn pardon. If I can stand before the King and claim that I have done something to win his favor, I am quite willing to come." But the herald replies,

"No; if you are pardoned, you must understand it is entirely and wholly as an act of grace on God's part. He sees nothing good in you, He knows that there is nothing good in you; He is willing to take you just as you are, black, and bad, and wicked, and undeserving; He is willing to give you graciously what He would not sell to you, and what He knows you cannot earn of Him. Will you have it?"

And naturally every man says, "No, I will not be saved in that style."

Well, then, soul, remember that thou wilt never be saved at all, for God's way is salvation by grace. You will have to confess if ever you are saved, my dear hearer, that you never deserved one single blessing from the God of grace; you will have to give all the glory to His holy name if ever you get to Heaven. And mark you, even in the matter of the acceptance of this offered mercy, you will never accept it unless He makes you willing. He does freely present it to every one of you, and He honestly bids you come to Christ and live; but you will never come, I know, except the effectual grace which first provided mercy shall make you willing to accept that mercy. So the text tells us it is His own purpose and grace.

6. Again, in order to shut out everything like boasting, the whole is spoken of as *a gift*. Do notice that; lest (for we are such straying sheep in this matter)—lest we should still slip out of the field, it is added, "purpose and grace which he gave us"—not "which He sold us," or "offered us," but "which He gave us." He must have a word here which shall be a death-blow to all merit—"Which He gave us"—it was given; and what can be more free than a gift, and what more evidently of grace?

7. But the gift is bestowed through a medium which glorifies Christ. It is written, "which was given us in Christ Jesus." We ask to have mercy from the well-head of grace, but we ask not even to make the bucket in which it is to be brought to us; Christ is to be the sacred vessel in which the grace of God is to be presented to our thirsty lips. Now where is boasting? Why surely there it sits at the foot of the cross and sings, "God forbid that I should glory save in the cross of our Lord Jesus Christ." Is it not grace and grace alone?

8. Yet further, a period is mentioned and added—"before the world began." Those last words seem to me forever to lay prostrate all idea of anything of our own merits in saving ourselves, because it is here witnessed that God gave us grace "before the world began." Where were you then? What hand had you in it "before the world began?"

Why, fly back if you can in imagination to the ancient years when those venerable mountains, that elder birth of nature, were not yet formed; when world, and sun, and moon, and stars, were all in embryo in God's great mind; when the unnavigated sea of space had never been disturbed by wings of seraph, and the awful silence of eternity had never been startled by the song of cherubim—when God dwelt alone. If you can conceive that time before all time, that vast eternity—it was then He gave us grace in Christ Jesus. What, Oh soul, hadst thou to do with that? Where were your merits then? Where were you? Oh thou small dust of the balance, thou insect of a day, where were you? See how Jehovah reigned, dispensing mercy as He would, and ordaining unto eternal life without taking counsel of man or angel, for neither man or angel then had an existence. That it might be all of grace He gave us grace before the world began.

I have honestly read out the doctrine of the text, and nothing more. If such is not the meaning of the text I do not know the meaning of it, and I cannot, therefore, tell you what it is, but I believe that I have given the natural and grammatical teaching of the text. If you do not like the doctrine, well, I cannot help it. I did not make the text, and if I have to expound it, I must expound it honestly as it is in my Master's Word, and I pray you to receive what He says whatever you may do with what I say.

USES OF THE DOCTRINE OF GRACE

I shall want your patience while I try to *show the uses of this doctrine*.

The doctrine of grace has been put by in the lumber chamber. It is acknowledged to be true, for it is confessed in most creeds; it is in the Church of England articles, it is in the confessions of all sorts of Protestant Christians—except those who are avowedly Arminian—but how little it is ever preached! It is put among the relics of the past. It is considered to be a respectable sort of retired officer, who is not expected to see any other active service. Now I believe that it is not a superannuated officer in the Master's army, but that it is full of force and vigor as ever.

But what is the use of it? Why, first then, it is clear from the connection that it has a tendency to embolden the man who receives it. Paul tells Timothy not to be ashamed, and he gives this as a motive: how can a man be ashamed when he believes that God has given him grace in Christ Jesus before the world was?

Suppose the man to be very poor. "Oh," says he, "what matters it? Though I have but a little oil in the cruse, and a little meal in the barrel, yet I have a lot and a portion in everlasting things. My name is not in Doomsday Book nor in Burke's Peerage; but it is in the book of God's election, and was there before the world began."

Such a man dares look the proudest of his fellows in the face. This was the doctrine on which the brave old Ironsides fed; the men who, when they rode to battle with the war-cry of "The Lord of hosts!" made the cavaliers fly before them like chaff before the wind. No doctrine like it for putting a backbone into a man, and making him feel that he is made for something better than to be trodden down like straw for the dunghill beneath a despot's heel. Sneer who will, the elect of God derive a nobility from the divine choice which no royal patent can outshine.

I wish that free grace were more preached, because it gives men something to believe with confidence. The great mass of professing Christians know nothing of doctrine; their religion consists in going a certain number of times to a place of worship, but they have no care for truth one way or another. I speak without any prejudice in this matter; but I have talked with a large number of persons in the course of my very extensive pastorate, who have been for years members of other churches, and when I have asked them a few questions upon doctrinal matters it did not seem to me that they were in error; they were perfectly willing to believe almost anything that any earnest man might teach them, but they did not know anything, they had no minds of their own, and no definite opinions. Our children, who have learned "The Westminster Assembly's

Confession of Faith," know more about the doctrines of grace and the doctrine of the Bible than hundreds of grown-up people who attend a ministry which very eloquently teaches nothing.

It was observed by a very excellent critic not long ago, that if you were to hear thirteen lectures on astronomy or geology, you might get a pretty good idea of what the science was, and the theory of the person who gave the lectures; but that if you were to hear thirteen hundred sermons from some ministers, you would not know at all what they were preaching about or what their doctrinal sentiments were. It ought not to be so. Is not this the reason why Puseyism[1] spreads so, and all sorts of errors have such a foothold, because our people as a whole do not know what they believe? The doctrines of the gospel, if well received, give to a man something which he knows and which he holds and which will become dear to him, for which he would be prepared to die if the first of persecution were again kindled.

Better still is it that this doctrine not only gives the man something to hold but it holds the man. Let a man once have burnt into him that salvation is of God and not of man, and that God's grace is to be glorified and not human merit, and you will never get that belief out of him; it is the rarest thing in all the world to hear of such a man ever apostatizing from his faith. Other doctrine is slippery ground, like the slope of a mountain composed of loose earth and rolling stones, down which the traveler may slide long before he can ever get a transient foothold; but

---

[1] Puseyism refers to the principles of Edward Pusey (1800-1882), a professor of Hebrew at Christ Church, Oxford English churchman who was influential in the so-called Oxford Movement, a movement whose members argued to reinstate Christian theology and practices closely aligned with Roman Catholicism into Anglicanism. The members of this movement thought of Anglicanism as one of the three branches (along with Roman Catholicism and Eastern Orthodox) of the "one, holy, catholic, and apostolic church."

this is like a granite step upon the eternal pyramid of truth; get your feet on this, and there is no fear of slipping so far as doctrinal standing in concerned. If we would have our churches in England well instructed and holding fast the truth, we must bring out the grand old verity of the eternal purpose of God in Christ Jesus before the world began. Oh, may the Holy Spirit write it on our hearts!

Moreover, my brethren, this doctrine overwhelms as with an avalanche all the claims of priest craft. Let it be told to men that they are saved by God, and they say at once, "Then what is the good of the priest?" If they are told it is God's grace then they say, "Then you do not want our money to buy masses and absolutions," and down goes the priest at once. Beloved, this is a battering ram that God uses with which to shake the gates of Hell. How much more forcible than the pretty essays of many divines, which have no more power than bulrushes, no more light than smoking flax.

What do you suppose people used to meet in woods for in persecuting times, meet by thousands outside the town of Antwerp, and such-like places on the Continent, in jeopardy of their lives? Do you suppose they would ever have come together to hear that poor milk-and-water theology of this age, or to receive the lukewarm milk and water of our modern anti-Calvinists? Not they, my brethren. They needed stronger meat, and more savory diet to attract them thus. Do you imagine that when it was death to listen to the preacher, men under the shadows of night, and amid the wings of tempest would then listen to philosophical essays, or to mere precepts, or to diluted, adulterated, soulless, theological suppositions? No, there is no energy in that kind of thing to draw men together under fear of their lives.

But what did bring them together in the dead of night amidst the glare of lightning, and the roll of thunder—what brought them together? Why, the doctrine of the grace of God, the doctrine of Jesus, and of His servants Paul, and Augustine, and Luther, and Calvin; for there is something in that doctrine which touches the heart of the Christian, and gives him food such as his soul loveth, savory meat, suitable to his heaven-born appetite. To hear this men braved death, and defied the sword. And if we are to see once again the scarlet hat plucked from the wearer's head, and the shaven crowns with all the gaudy trumpery of Rome sent back to the place from whence they came—and Heaven grant that they make take our Puseyite Established Church with them—it must be by declaring the doctrines of the grace of God. When these are declared and vindicated in every place, we shall yet again make these enemies of God and man to know that they cannot stand their ground for a moment, where men of God wield the sword of the Lord and of Gideon by preaching the doctrines of the grace of God.

Brethren, let the man receive these truths; let them be written in his heart by the Holy Spirit, and they will make him look up. He will say, "God has saved me;" and he will walk with a constant eye to God. He will not forget to see the hand of God in nature and in providence; he will, on the contrary, discern the Lord working in all places, and will humbly adore Him. He will not give to laws of nature or schemes of state the glory due to the most High, but will have respect unto the unseen Ruler. "What the Lord saith to me that will I do," is the believer's language. "What is His will that will I follow; what is His Word, that will I believe; what is His promise, on that I will live." It is a blessed habit to teach a man to look up, look up to God in all things.

At the same time this doctrine makes a man look down upon himself. "Ah," saith he, "I am nothing; there is nothing in me to merit esteem. I have no goodness of my own. If saved, I cannot praise myself; I cannot in any way ascribe to myself honor; God has done it, God has done it." Nothing makes the man so humble; but nothing makes him so glad; nothing lays him so low at the mercy seat, but nothing makes him so brave to look his fellow man in the face. It is a grand truth: would God ye all knew its mighty power!

Lastly, this precious truth is full of comfort to the sinner, and that is why I love it. As it has been preached by some it has been exaggerated and made into a boogeyman. Why, there are some who preach the doctrine of election as though it were a line of sharp pikes to keep a sinner from coming to Christ, as though it were a sharp, glittering halberd to be pushed into the breast of a coming sinner to keep him from mercy. Now it is not so.

Sinner, whoever you may be, your greatest comfort should be to know that salvation is by grace. Why, man, if it were by merit, what would become of you? Suppose that God saved men on account of their merits, where would you drunkards be? Where would you swearers be? You who have been unclean and unchaste, and you whose hearts have cursed God, and who even now do not love Him, where would you be? But when it is all of grace, why then all your past life, however black and filthy it may be, need not keep you from coming to Jesus.

Christ receiveth sinners, God has elected sinners; He has elected some of the blackest of sinners—why not you? He receives every one that comes to Him. He will not cast out. There have been some who have hated Him, insulted him to His face, that have burned His servants alive, and have persecuted Him in His members, but as soon as even they have cried, "God be merciful to me a sinner," He has given them mercy at once, and He will give it to you if you be led to seek it. If I had to tell you that you were to work out your own salvation apart from His grace it were a sad look-out for you, but when it comes to you thus: black, there is washing for you! Dead! There is life for you! Naked! There is raiment for you! All undone and ruined! Here is a complete salvation for you! Oh soul, mayest thou have grace to lay hold of it, and then thou and I together will sing to the praise of the glory of divine grace.

4

How Is Salvation Received?[1]

"Therefore it is of faith, that it might be by Grace; to the end the promise might be sure to all the seed; not to that only which is of the Law, but to that, also, which is of the faith of Abraham; who is the father of us all" (Romans 4:16).

W E SHALL TURN DURING yet another Sabbath morning to one of the great vital Truths of the Gospel. I feel it to be more and more important to bring forward the fundamental doctrines since they are, in certain quarters, placed so much in the background. I met with a remark the other day that even the evangelical pulpit needs to be evangelized—I am afraid it is too true and, therefore, we will give such prominence to the Gospel and to its central doctrine of Justification by Faith, that no such remark shall be applicable to us. We have heard it said that if an instrument could be invented which would serve the same purpose towards sermons as the lactometer does towards milk, you would, with great difficulty, be able to discover any trace of the unadulterated milk of the Word of God in large numbers of modern discourses.

---

[1] A sermon delivered by C. H. Spurgeon on April 1, 1877 at the Metropolitan Tabernacle, Newington.

I shall not subscribe to any sweeping censure, but I am afraid there is too much ground for the accusation. In abundance of sermons, the polish of the rhetoric is greatly in excess of the weight of the doctrine and "the wisdom of words" is far more conspicuous than the Cross of Christ.

Besides, the Gospel is always needed. There are always some persons who urgently need it and will perish unless they receive it. It is a matter of hourly necessity! There may be finer and more artistic things to speak about than the simplicities of Christ, but there are certainly no more useful and requisite things.

The signposts at the crossroads bear very simple words, generally consisting of the names of the towns and villages to which the roads lead. But if these were painted out and their places supplied with stanzas from Byron, or stately lines from Milton, or deep thoughts from Cowper or Young, I am afraid there would be grievous complaints from persons losing their way! They would declare that however excellent the poetry might be, they thought it an impertinence to mock them with a verse when they needed plain directions as to the king's highway! So let those who will, indulge in poetical thoughts and express them in high-flown language—it shall be ours to set up the signposts marking out the way of salvation and to keep them painted in letters large and plain—so that he who runs may read.

There is another reason for giving the Gospel over and over, again and again. It is the reason which makes the mother tell her child 20 times, namely, because 19 times are not enough! Men are so forgetful about the things of Christ and their minds are so apt to step aside from the Truth of God, that when they have learned the Gospel they are very easily bewitched by falsehood and are readily deceived by that "other gospel" which is not another! Therefore, we need to give them "line upon line and precept upon precept." I scarcely remember the old rustic rhyme, but I remember hearing it sung in my boyish days when the country people were planting beans according to the old plan of putting three into each hole—I think it ran thus—"One for the worm and one for the crow, And let us hope the other will grow."

We must be content to plant many seeds in the hope that one will take root and bear fruit! The worm and crow are always at work and will be sure to get their full share of our sowing and, therefore, let us sow the more! Come we, then, to our text and to the Gospel of faith. Last Lord's Day the theme was, "For whom is the Gospel meant?" And the reply was, *for sinners*. The question, today, is, "How is the Gospel received?" The answer is, *by faith*. Our first head shall be the fact—"it is of faith." Secondly, the first reason for this—"that it might be by Grace." And thirdly, the further reason—"to the end that the promise might be sure to all the seed."

IT IS OF FAITH

First, then, here is *the fact*—it is of faith. What does the "it" refer to? It is of faith. If you will read the context, I think you will consider that it refers to the promise, although some have said that the antecedent word or thought is, "the inheritance." This matters very little, if at all—it may mean the inheritance, the Covenant, or the promise, for these are one. To give a wide word which will take in all—the blessedness which comes to a man in Christ, the blessedness promised by the Covenant of Grace is of faith—in one word, salvation is of faith!

And what is faith? It is believing the promise of God, taking God at His word and acting upon that belief by trusting in Him. Some of the Puritans used to divide faith improperly, but still instructively, into three parts. The *first* was self-renunciation, which is, perhaps, rather a preparation for faith than faith itself. In it a man confesses that he cannot trust in himself and so goes out of self and all confidence in his own good

69

works. The *second* part of faith, they said, was reliance in which a man, believing the promise of God, trusts Him, depends upon Him and leaves his soul in the Savior's hands. And then they said the *third* part of faith was appropriation by which a man takes to himself that which God presents in the promise to the Believer—he appropriates it as his own, feeds upon it and enjoys it.

Certainly there is no true faith without self-renunciation, reliance and at least a measure of appropriation—where these three are found, there is faith in the soul. We shall, however, better understand what faith is as we proceed with our subject, if God the Holy Spirit will be pleased to enlighten us. Dear Friends, you can easily see that the blessing was of faith in Abraham's case—and it is precisely the same with all those who, by faith, are the children of believing Abraham!

First, it was so in the case of Abraham. Abraham obtained the promise by faith and not by works nor by the energy of the flesh. He relied alone upon the Divine promise. We read in the 17th verse—"(As it is written, I have made you a father of many nations), before Him whom he believed, even God, who quickens the dead and calls those things which are not as though they were." Abraham's faith consisted in believing the promise of God and this he did firmly and practically. He was far away in Chaldea when the Lord called him out and promised to give him a land and a seed. And straightway he went forth, not knowing where he went. When he came into Canaan, he had no settled resting place, but wandered about in tents, still believing most fully that the land in which he sojourned as a stranger was his own.

God promised to give him a seed and yet he had no children. Year followed year and in the course of nature he grew old and his wife was long past the age of child-bearing—and yet there was no son born to them. When at last Ishmael was born, his hope in that direction was dashed to the ground, for he was informed that the Covenant was not with Ishmael—believing Abraham had stepped aside to carnal expediency and had hoped, in that way, to realize the lingering promise! But he had 14 more years to wait—till he was 100 years old and till Sarah had reached her 90th year! Yet he believed the word of the Lord and fell upon his face and laughed with holy joy and said in his heart, "Shall a child be born unto him that is 100 years old?"

So, too, when Isaac was born and grown up, he believed that in Isaac should the Covenant be established. Nor did he doubt this when the Lord commanded him to take Isaac and offer him up as a sacrifice! He obeyed without questioning, believing that God was able to raise Isaac from the dead, or in some other way to keep His word of promise (Heb. 11:17-19).

Now consider that we have multiplied promises and those are written down in black and white in the Inspired Word, which we may consult at any time we please, while Abraham had only, now and then, a verbal promise—and yet he clung to it and relied upon it. Though there was nothing else to rely upon and neither sign nor evidence of any offspring to fulfill the promise that he should be heir of the world and father of many nations, yet he needed no other ground of confidence but that God had said it and that He would make His word good. There was in Abraham, also, an eye to the central point of the promise—the Messiah—Jesus, our Lord.

I do not know that Abraham understood all the spiritual meaning of the Covenant made with him. Probably he did not. But he did understand that the Christ was to be born of him, in whom all nations should be blessed. When the Lord said that He would make him a blessing and in him should all nations of the earth be blessed, I do not suppose Abraham saw all the fullness of that marvelous word—but he did see that he was to be the progenitor of the Messiah. Our Lord, Himself, is my Authority for this assertion—"Abraham saw My day, he saw it and was glad" (John 8:56). Though there appeared to this man, old

71

and withered, with a wife 90 years of age, no likelihood that he should ever become a father, yet did he fully believe that he would be the father of many nations—and that upon no basis whatever but that the living God had so promised him and, therefore, so it must be!

This faith of Abraham we find considered no difficulties whatever.

"Who against hope believed in hope, that he might become the father of many nations, according to that which was spoken, So shall your seed be. And being not weak in faith, he considered not his own body now dead, when he was about 100 years old, neither yet the deadness of Sarah's womb: he staggered not at the promise of God through unbelief."

Brothers and Sisters, these were, in themselves, terrible difficulties—enough to make a man fear that the promise did but mock him—but Abraham did not consider anything beyond the promise and the God who gave it! The difficulties were for God to consider—not for him! He knew that God had made the world out of nothing and that He supported all things by the word of His power and, therefore, he felt that nothing was too hard for Him!

His own advanced years and the age of his wife were of no consequence. He did not take them into the reckoning, but saw only a faithful Almighty God and felt content. Oh noble faith! Faith such as God deserves! Faith such as none render to Him but those whom He calls by Irresistible Grace! This it was which justified Abraham and made him the father of Believers! Abraham's faith, also, gave glory to God. I stopped in the middle of the 20th verse just now, but we must now complete the reading of it. "But was strong in faith, giving glory to God." God had promised and he treated the Lord's promise with becoming reverence.

He did not impiously suspect the Lord of falsehood, or of mocking His servant, or of uttering today what He might take back tomorrow.

Abraham knew that Jehovah is not a man, that He should lie, nor the son of man that He should repent. Abraham glorified the Truth of God and, at the same time, he glorified His power! He was quite certain that the Lord had not spoken beyond His line, but that what He had promised He was able to perform. It belongs to puny man to speak more than he can do—full often his tongue is longer than his arm—but with the Lord it is never so. Has He said, and shall He not do it? Is anything too hard for the Lord? Abraham adoringly believed in the immutability, truth and power of the living God—and looked for the fulfillment of His words!

All this strong, unstaggering faith which glorified God rested upon the Lord alone. You will see that it was so by reading the 21st verse. "Being fully persuaded that, what He had promised, He was able, also, to perform." There was nothing whatever in his house, his wife, himself, or anywhere else which could guarantee the fulfillment of the promise. He had only God to look to—*only*, did I say?—What could a man have more? Yet so it was. There were no signs, marks, tokens, or indications to substantiate the confidence of Abraham! He rested solely upon the unlimited power of God! And this, dear Brothers and Sisters, is the kind of faith which God loves and honors—which needs no signs, marks, evidences, helps, or other buttresses to support the plain and sure Word of the Lord—but simply knows that Jehovah has said it and that He will make it good!

Though all things should give the promise the lie, we believe in it because we believe in God. True faith ridicules impossibility and pours contempt upon improbability, knowing that Omnipotence and Immutability cannot be thwarted or hindered. Has God said it? Then so it is! Dictum! Factum! Spoken! Done! These two are one with the Most

High! Well, now, the faith of every man who is saved must be of this character. Every man who receives salvation receives it by a faith like that of Abraham, for, my Brothers and Sisters, when we are saved we, too, take the promise of God and depend upon it! To one Believer, one Word of God is applied. To another, some sweet Word, most sure and steadfast, is discovered upon which we fix our hope and find an anchor for our spirit. Yes, and as we search the Word by faith—we take each promise as we find it and we say, "this is true," and, "this is true," and so we rest upon all of them!

Is it not so with all of you who have peace with God? Did you not gain it by resting upon the promises of God as you found it in the Word and as it was opened up to you by the Holy Spirit? Have you any other ground of confidence but God's promise? I know you have not, my Brethren, nor do you desire any! And we, also, believe in God over the head of great difficulties. If it were difficult for Abraham to believe that a son should be born to him, I think it is harder for a poor burdened sinner, conscious of his great guilt—conscious that God must punish him, also, for that guilt—to believe, nevertheless, in the hopeful things which the Gospel prophesies unto him!

Can I believe that the righteous God is looking upon me, a sinner, with eyes of love? Can I believe that though I have offended Him and broken all His Laws, He, nevertheless, waits to be gracious to me? While my heart is heavy and the prospect is black around me and I see nothing but a terrible Hell to be my eternal portion—can I, at such a time, believe that God has planned my redemption and given His Son to die for me— and that now He invites me to come and receive a full, perfect and immediate pardon at His hands? Can the Gospel message be true to such a worthless rebel as I am?

It seems as if the Law and Justice of God set themselves against the truth of such wonderful deeds of mercy as the Gospel announces! And it is hard for a stricken heart to believe the report—but the faith which saves the soul believes the Gospel promise in the teeth of all its alarms and, notwithstanding, all the thunders of the Law! Despite the trepidation of the awakened spirit, the Holy Spirit enables it to accept the great Father's promise, to rest upon the propitiation which He has set forth and to quiet itself with the firm persuasion that God, for Christ's sake, does put away its sin.

At the same time another grand miracle is also believed in, namely, regeneration. This seems to me to be quite as great an act of faith as for Abraham to believe in the birth of a child by two parents who were both advanced in years. The case stands thus—here am I, dead by nature— dead in trespasses and sins. The deadness of Abraham and Sarah, according to nature, was not greater than the deadness of my soul to every good thing. Is it possible, then, that I should live unto God? That within this stony heart there should yet throb eternal life and Divine Love? That I should come to delight in God? Can it be that with such a depraved and deceitful heart as mine should yet rise to fellowship with the holy God and should call Him my Father and feel the spirit of adoption within my heart?

Can I, who now dread the Lord, yet come to rejoice in Him? "Oh," says the poor troubled sinner, "can I, that have fought against the Throne of God. I that even tried to doubt His existence—can I ever come to be at perfect peace with Him so that He shall call me His *friend* and reveal His secrets to me and listen to my voice in prayer? Is it possible?" The faith which saves the soul believes in the possibility of regeneration and sanctification—no, more—it believes in Jesus and obtains for us power to become children of God and strength to conquer sin! This is believing God, indeed!

Look this way, yet again, for here is another difficulty. We know that we must persevere to the end, for only he that endures to the end shall be saved. Does it not seem incredible that such feeble, fickle, foolish creatures as we are should continue in faith and the fear of God all our lives? Yet this we must do! The faith which saves, enables us to believe that we shall persevere, for it is persuaded that the Redeemer is able to keep that which we have committed unto Him, that He will perfect that which concerns us, that He will suffer none to pluck us out of His hands and that having begun the good work in us He will carry it on! This is faith worthy of the father of the faithful!

Once again, let us behold another difficulty for faith. We believe, according to God's promise, that we shall one day be "without spot or wrinkle, or any such thing." I do believe that this head shall wear a crown of glory and that this hand shall wave a palm branch. I am fully assured that He will one day sweetly say to me—

> "Close your eyes that you may see
> What I have in store for thee.
> Lay your arms of warfare down,
> Fall that you may win a crown."

We, all, who are Believers in Jesus, shall one day be without fault before the Throne of God! But how is this to be? Surely our confidence is that He who has promised it is able to perform it! This is the faith which finds its way to Glory—the faith which expects to enter into the Redeemer's joy because of the Redeemer's love and life!

Brothers and Sisters, in this matter we see the difficulties, but we do not consider them—we count them as less than nothing since Omnipotence has come into the field. "Thanks be unto God which gives us the victory through our Lord Jesus Christ." We know that our Redeemer lives and that because He lives, we shall, also—live and be with Him where He is! At the end of the chapter we are told that this saving faith rests in the power of God as manifested in Jesus—"If we believe in Him who was delivered for our offenses, and was raised again for our justification." Beloved, we believe that Jesus died, as certainly died as ever any man died—and yet on the morning of the third day He rose again from the dead by Divine power.

It is not, to us, an incredible thing that God should raise the dead! We, therefore, believe that because God has raised the dead, He has raised us also from our death in sin and that He will raise our bodies from the tomb after they shall have slept, awhile, in the earth. We believe, also, that our Lord Jesus died for our offenses and put them away. Our faith builds upon the substitution of the Lord Jesus on our behalf and it rests there with firm confidence. We believe, also, that He rose again because His substitution was accepted and because our offenses were forever put away—rose again to prove that we are justified in Him! This is where we stand! I expect to be saved, not at all because of what I am, nor of what I can do, nor because of anything I ever shall be able to be or to do—but only because God has promised to save those who believe in Jesus Christ through what the Lord Jesus has suffered in their place.

Because Jesus has risen to prove that His suffering was accepted on the behalf of Believers, there do we rest and trust, and that is the way in which every Believer is saved—that way and no way else. Even as Abraham believed, so do we! Here is the fact—it is of faith.

THE REASON FOR FAITH

Now we come to the second point. Here we are to consider *the first reason* why God has chosen to make salvation by faith, "that it might be of Grace." Now, dear Friends, the Lord might have willed to make the condition of salvation a mitigated form of works. If He had done so, it would not have been of Grace, for it is a principle which I need not explain now, but a fixed principle, that if the blessing is of Grace it is no more of works, otherwise Grace is no more Grace. And if it is of works, it is no more of Grace, otherwise work is no more work.

As water and oil will not mix, and as fire and water will not lie down side by side in quiet, so neither will the principle of merit and the principle of free favor. You cannot make a legal work to be a condition of a gracious blessing without at once introducing an alien element and really bringing the soul under the Covenant of Works and so spoiling the whole plan of mercy! Grace and faith are congruous and will draw together in the same chariot, but Grace and merit are contrary, the one to the other, and pull opposite ways and, therefore, God has not chosen to yoke them together. He will not build with incongruous materials or daub with untempered mortar. He will not make an image partly of gold and partly of clay, nor weave a linsey-woolsey garment—His work is all of one piece and that one piece is all Grace!

Again, in Abraham's case, inasmuch as he received, by faith, the blessing which God promised him, it is very evident that it was of Grace. You never heard anyone ascribe Abraham's salvation to his merits and yet Abraham was an eminently holy man. There are specks in his life— and in whose life will there not be found infirmities?—but he was one of the grandest characters of history. Still, no man thinks of Abraham as a self-justifying person, or as at all related to the Pharisee who said, "God, I thank You that I am not as other men." I never heard anybody hint that the great Patriarch had reason to glory before God. His name is not "the father of the innocent," but, "the father of the faithful." When we read of Abraham's life, we see that God called him by an act of Sovereign Grace, made a Covenant with him as an act of Grace and that the promised child was born—not of the power of the flesh, but entirely according to promise. Grace reigns through righteousness unto eternal life in the life of the Patriarch and it is illustrated in a thousand ways whenever we see his faith receiving the promises! The holiness of Abraham, since it arose out of his faith, never leads us to ascribe his blessedness to anything but the Grace of God!

Now, inasmuch as we are saved by faith, every Believer is made to see in himself that, in his own instance, it is by Grace. Believing is such a self-renounciating act that no man who looks for eternal life thereby ever talked about his own merits except to count them but dross and dung. No, Brothers and Sisters, the child of the promise cannot live in the same house with the son of the bondwoman. When Isaac grows up, Ishmael must depart—the principle of believing unto everlasting life will not endure a hint about human merit. Those who believe in Justification by Faith are the only persons who can believe in salvation by Grace!

The Believer may grow in Grace till he becomes fully assured of his own salvation, yes, and he may become holiness unto the Lord in a very remarkable manner, being wholly consecrated to God in body, soul and spirit. But you will never hear the believing man speak of his experience, or attainments, or achievements as a reason for glorying in himself, or as an argument for becoming more confident as to his safety. He dares not trust his works, or states of feeling, for he feels that he stands by faith. He cannot get away from simple faith, for the moment he attempts to do so, he feels the ground going from under him and he begins to sink into horrible confusion of spirit. Therefore he returns to his rest and resolves to abide in faith in his risen Savior, for there he abides in the Grace of God.

Through the prominence given to faith, the Truth of God of salvation by Grace is so conspicuously revealed that even the outside world is compelled to see it, though the only result may be to make them raise trivial objections. They charge us with preaching too much concerning Grace because they hear us magnifying and extolling the plan of salvation by faith. They readily perceive that a gift promised to faith must be a gift of Grace and not a reward for services done. Only begin to preach salvation by works or ceremonies and nobody will accuse you of saying too much of Grace! But keep to faith and you are sure to keep to the preaching of Grace!

Moreover, faith never did clash with Grace. When the sinner comes and trusts Christ and Christ says to him, "I forgive you freely by My Grace," Faith says, "Oh Lord, that is what I need and what I believe in. I ask You to deal with me even so." "But if I give you everlasting life, it will not be because you deserve it, but for My own name's sake." Faith replies, "Oh Lord, that, also, is precisely as I desire! It is the sum and substance of my prayer."

When Faith grows strong and takes to pleading in prayer (and oh how mighty she is with God in supplication, moving His Omnipotence to her mind), yet all her pleadings are based on Grace—none of them upon the merit of the creature! Never yet did Faith borrow weapons from Mount Sinai! Never once did she ask as though the favor were a debt, but she always holds to the promise of the gracious God and expects all things from the faithfulness of her God. Yes, and when Faith grows strongest and attains to her highest stature and is most full of delight, so that she dances for very joy, yet she never, in all her exultation, boasts or exalts herself!

Where is boasting, then? It is excluded! By the Law of works? No, but by the Law of faith! Faith and carnal boasting never yet walked together! If a man should boast of the strength of his faith, it would be clear evidence that he had none at all, or at least that he had, for the time, fallen into vainglorious presumption. Boasting? No, Faith loves to lie low and behave herself as a little child. And when she lifts herself up, it is to exalt her Lord, and her Lord, alone.

Faith, too, is well calculated to show forth the Grace of God, because Faith is the child of Grace. "Ah," says Faith, "I have grasped the

Covenant. I have laid hold on the promises, I have seen Christ, I have gazed into Heaven, I have enjoyed foretastes of eternal joys! But (she says) I am of the operation of God—I would never have existed if the Spirit of God had not created me!" The Believer knows that his faith is not a weed suitable to the soil of his heart, but a rare plant—an exotic which has been planted there by Divine Wisdom—and he knows, too, that if the Lord does not nourish it, his faith will die like a withered flower.

He knows that his faith is a perpetual miracle, for it is begotten, sustained and preserved by a power not less mighty than that which raised our Lord Jesus Christ from the dead! If I met with an angel in a hovel I should know that he was not born there, but that he came from above. And so is it with faith—its heavenly descent is manifest to all! Faith, then, tracing her very existence to Grace, never can be anything but the friend, the vindicator, the advocate and the glorifier of the Grace of God—therefore it is of faith that it might be by Grace!

STILL ANOTHER REASON FOR FAITH

Now, thirdly, there is *a further reason* for faith and Grace being the Lord's chosen method of salvation—"To the end that the promise might be sure to all the seed." Look at this, dear Friends, very carefully. Salvation was made to be of faith and not of works that the promise might be sure to all the seed, for first, it could not have been sure to us Gentiles by the Law, because in a certain sense we were not under the Law of Moses at all. Turn to the text and you find that it runs thus— "Sure to all the seed, not to that only which is of the Law, but to that, also, which is of the faith of Abraham, who is the father of us all."

That is to say, the Jew, receiving the seal of circumcision and coming under the ceremonial Law, eating its Passover and presenting its

81

sacrifices, might possibly have been reached by a legal method. But we who are Gentiles would have been altogether shut out. As to the Covenant according to the flesh, we are aliens and have never come under its bonds or participated in its privileges and, therefore, Grace chooses to bless us by faith in order that the Gentile may partake of the blessing of the Covenant as well as the Jew.

But there is a still wider reason—it is of faith because the other method has failed, already, in every case. We have all broken the Law and so have put ourselves beyond the power of ever receiving blessing as a reward of merit. Failure at the outset has ruined our future prospects— and from now on—by the deeds of the Law shall no flesh be justified. What remains, then, if we are to be saved at all, but that it should be of faith? This door, alone, is open! Let us bless God that no man can shut it!

Again, it is of faith that it might be sure. Now, under the system of works nothing is sure.

Suppose, my dear Brothers and Sisters, you were under a Covenant of salvation by works and you had fulfilled those works up till now, yet you would not be sure. Are you 70 years of age and have you kept your standing till now? Well, you have done a great deal more than father Adam did, for though he was a perfect man without any natural corruption, I do not suppose that he kept his first estate for a day. But after all you have done for these long years you may lose everything before you have finished your next meal! If your standing depends upon your own works, you are not safe and can never be safe till you are out of this present life, for you might sin and that one offense against the conditions would destroy the Covenant! "When the righteous turns from his righteousness and commits iniquity, he shall even die thereby."

But see the excellence of salvation by Grace—when you reach the ground of faith in the promises, you are upon *terra firma*, and your soul is no longer in jeopardy. Here is a sure foundation, for the Divine promise cannot fail! If my salvation depends upon the Lord and is received by me on the ground that the Lord has decreed it, promised it in Covenant and ensured it to me by the blood of Jesus Christ, then it is so mine that neither life nor death nor Satan nor the world shall ever rob me of it! If I live to the age of Methuselah, my faith will have the same promises to rest upon—and clinging there she will defy the lapse of years to change her immutable security.

The promise would not be sure to one of the seed by any other means than that of Grace through faith, but now it is sure to all the seed. Moreover, if the promise had been made to works, there are some of the seed to whom, most evidently, it never could come. One of the seed of Abraham hung dying upon a cross and within an hour or two his bones were broken that he might the more quickly die and be buried. Now, if salvation to that poor dying thief must come by works, how can he be saved? His hands and feet are fastened up and he is in the very grip of death—what can he do? The promise would not have been sure to him, my Brothers and Sisters, if there had been any active condition! But he believed, cast a saving eye upon the Lord Jesus and said, "Lord, remember me," and the promise was most sure to him, for the answer was—"Today shall you be with Me in Paradise!"

Many a chosen one of God is brought into such a condition that nothing is possible to him except faith, but Grace has made the act of believing divinely possible. Well was it for those bitten by serpents that all that was asked of them was a look, for this was possible even when the hot venom made the blood boil and scalded all the frame with fever! Faith is possible to the blind, the lame, the deaf, the dumb! Faith is possible to the almost-idiot, the desponding and the guilty! Faith can be possessed by babes and by the extremely aged, by the illiterate as well as by the instructed! It is well chosen as the cup to convey the living water, for it is not too heavy for the weak, nor too huge for the little, nor too small for the full-grown.

Now, Brothers and Sisters, I have done when I have said just this. I will ask you who have believed in Christ, one question—you who are resting in the promise of God, you who are depending upon the finished work of Him who was delivered for your offenses—how do you feel? Are you rejoicing in your unquestionable safety? As I have turned this matter over and thought upon it, my soul has dwelt in perfect peace! I cannot conceive anything that God Himself could give to the Believer which would make him safer than the work of Christ has made him. God cannot lie! Are you not sure of this?

He must keep His promises! Are you not certain of this? What more do you need? As a little child believes its father's words without any question, even so should we rest on the bare, naked promise of Jehovah! And in so doing we become conscious of a peace that passes all understanding, which keeps our hearts and minds by Christ Jesus.

I dare not say otherwise, nor be silent, for I am conscious of being able to say—"therefore being justified by faith, I have peace with God." In that place of the soul, much love springs up and inward unity to God and conformity to Christ. Faith believes her God and trusts Him for time and eternity, for little things and great things, for body and for soul and this leads on to still higher results! Oh blessed God, what a union of desire, heart and aim exists between You and the soul that trusts You! How are we brought into harmony with Your mind and purposes! How is our heart made to delight in You! How completely is our soul "bound up in the bundle of life with the soul of the Lord our God!"

We grow up into Him in all things who is our Head, our Life, our All. I charge you, dear children of God, "As you have received Christ Jesus the Lord, so walk in Him." Live in His peace and abound in it more and more. Do not be afraid of being too peaceful, "rejoice in the Lord always, and again I say rejoice." When you have to condemn yourself for shortcomings, yet do not question the promises of the Lord! When sin overcomes you, confess the fault, but do not doubt the pardon which Jesus still gives you! When sharp temptations and severe trials arise from different quarters, do not suffer them to carry you by storm—let not the stronghold and castle of your spirit be captured—"let not your heart be troubled." Stagger not at the promise through unbelief, but hold to it whether you walk in the sunshine or in Egyptian darkness. That which the Lord has promised He is able, also, to perform. Do not doubt it! Lean hard on the faithful promise and when you feel sad at heart, lean harder and harder still, for, "faithful is He that has promised, who, also, will do it."

Last of all, you sinners here this morning who have heard all about this salvation by trusting—I charge you do not rest till you have trusted the Lord Jesus Christ and rested in the great promises of God. Here is one—"I will be merciful to their unrighteousness, and their sins and their iniquities will I remember no more forever." Here is another which is very cheering—"Whoever calls upon the name of the Lord shall be saved." Call upon Him in prayer and then say, "Lord, I have called, and You have said I shall be saved." Here is another gracious word—"He that believes and is baptized shall be saved." Attend you to these two commands and then say, "Lord, I have Your Word for it that I shall be saved, and I hold You to it." Believe God, Sinner!

Oh that He would give you Grace this morning, by His Holy Spirit, to say, "How can I do otherwise than believe Him? I dare not doubt Him." Oh poor tried Soul, believe in Jesus so as to trust your guilty soul with Him. The more guilty you feel yourself to be, the more is it in your power to glorify God by believing that He can forgive and renew such a guilty one as you are! If you lie buried like a fossil in the lowest stratum of sin, yet He can quarry for you and fetch you up out of the horrible pit—and make your dry, petrified heart live! Do you believe this?

"If you can believe, all things are possible to him that believes." Trust the promise that He makes to every Believer that He will save him! Hold to it, for it is not a vain thing! It is your life! "But what if I obtain no joy or peace?" Still, believe the promise, and joy and peace will come. "But what if I see no signs?" Ask for no signs! Be willing to trust God's Word without any other guarantee but His truthful Character and you will thus give Him glory. "Blessed are they that have not seen and yet have believed." Believe that Jehovah cannot lie and as He has promised to forgive all who believe in Jesus, hang on to that Word and you *shall be* saved! Sinners, I have set before you the way of salvation as simply as I can, will you have it or not? May the Spirit of God sweetly lead you to say, "Have it? Yes, that I will." Then go in peace and rejoice from now on and forever! God bless you. Amen.

5
Salvation As It Is Now Received[1]

"Whom having not seen, ye love; in whom, though now ye see him not, yet believing, ye rejoice with joy unspeakable and full of glory: receiving the end of your faith, even the salvation of your souls" (1 Peter 1:8-9).

W E USUALLY SPEAK OF the greater benefits of salvation as being in the future. We desire that we may be found in Christ in the day of his appearing, and that we may have a share in his eternal glory. But, beloved, salvation is not another a thing of the future; it is very decidedly a present matter, a blessing to be possessed now, and to be enjoyed now, and our text brings out that idea very clearly. Peter does not write about the elect strangers hoping to receive salvation by-and-by; but putting it all in the present tense, he says, "Whom having not seen, ye love; believing, ye rejoice . . . receiving the end of your faith, even the salvation of your souls." The perfection of salvation is reserved for the second coming of the Lord; for, at present, the body is mortal because of sin, it is subject to pain, and it will die, unless the Lord should first come, and it will for a while lie in the grave. But, at his appearing shall be a resurrection of the body, and then body

---

[1] A sermon delivered by C. H. Spurgeon on June 23, 1872 at the Metropolitan Tabernacle, Newington.

and soul reunited shall experience the fullness of salvation. In that respect, therefore, salvation still remains in part a matter for the future; yet, with the true child of God, the essence of salvation is a thing of today.

Even now, we rejoice with joy unspeakable and full of glory, receiving the end of our faith, even the salvation of our souls. I am going to speak upon this matter in the following way. First, we will enquire, what part of salvation do we receive here and now? Secondly, how do we now receive salvation? And then, thirdly we will make the solemn enquiry for all here. Namely, have we received salvation, and, if so, how far have we gone in the reception of it?

THE HERE AND NOW

My first question is, *what part of salvation do we receive here and now*? My first answer to the question is that, in a certain sense, we already possess the whole of it, for all salvation is wrapped up in Christ, and Christ is ours if we are truly believing in him. He is this day our Savior and our All-in-All; and he is already made unto us wisdom, and righteousness, and sanctification, and redemption. There is nothing of salvation that is outside of Christ; and therefore, since Christ is ours, the whole of salvation is ours. It is ours by the grip of faith, and the grace of hope, that living hope which is sure of realization, that well-grounded hope, which, cannot be disappointed. Our expectation is of so vivid a character that, it brings, not only near to us, but, into actual present possession, joys which as yet are not revealed; so again I say that, in a sense, it is true for us to say that we have received, in faith and hope, the salvation of our souls if we have truly believed in Jesus; for, "The moment a sinner believes, and trusts in his crucified God, His pardon at once he receives, Redemption in full through Christ's blood."

But, secondly, if we are to answer the question distinctly, and in detail, we should say that, if we have really trusted in Jesus, we have so far received the salvation of our souls that we have at this moment, the assurance of the perfect pardon of all our sins. Let me repeat those words: if we have really believed in Jesus, we have, at this moment, the assurance of the perfect pardon of all our sins. And I will venture to put, it as strongly as this, and to say that yonder white-robed spirits before the eternal throne are not more clear of the guilt of sin before the bar of infallible justice than was the dying thief the very moment that he turned his eye in faith to Christ upon the cross of Calvary, or than you are if you are now trusting to the same Savior, or than I am as now depending alone upon the blood and righteousness of Jesus Christ, my Lord and Savior. The pardon which God gives to believers in Jesus is not a semi-pardon, it is not a putting away of some of their sins, or a putting them away for a time; but it is a perfect putting away of their sins forever, a casting of them, once for all, behind God's back, into the depths of the sea, so that they shall never be found again; yea, they shall be so completely put away that they shall cease to be, according to that divine declaration, "The iniquity of Israel shall be sought for, and there shall be none."

Oh, what a glorious truth is this, that, although a poor tried child of God may feel the force of his inbred sin, and have continually to struggle with, it; and though he may, from day to day, be conscious of his many imperfections, yet, before those eyes that see everything, there is no spot, to be seen upon the believer in Christ—I mean, no spot in this respect, that he can ever be condemned or punished for his sin. His sin is finally and forever pardoned. God has blotted it out, like a cloud that has been blown away and completely dispersed. Therefore, let our spirits rejoice if we are truly trusting in Jesus; and oh, that some, who have never done so before, would now look believingly unto him! If they do thus look, this moment, they shall obtain perfect pardon, and so shall receive the end of their faith, even the salvation of their souls. I cannot help repeating that sweet verse of Kent's which I have often repeated to you, which sounds so strange, but which is, I believe, absolutely true:

> "Here's pardon for transgressions past,
>   It matters not how black their cast;
> And, O my soul, with wonder view,
>   For sins to come here's pardon too."

And next, beloved, we have received the salvation of our souls in this sense, that the alienation of our hearts from God is now effectually removed. We are saved from that alienation, and that is a very great part of salvation. Once, our backs were turned towards God; but now, our faces are turned towards him. At one time, we did not admire his character, nor desire, to imitate him, nor wish for his friendship, nor perhaps even so much as think of his existence, much less did we aspire to give him glory.

But now, having believed in Jesus, we have undergone a complete change. We are not yet what, we ought to be; we are still a long way off what we expect one day to be, yet we do desire to be what we should be. We admire the character of God, even though we have to prostrate ourselves in the dust when we see how far our own character is from likeness to it, and the whole set and current of our desires is towards purity and holiness. If we could have our way, our way should not be a sinful one. If our will could be gratified, our will would be that God should have his will with us, and that we should be in all things conformed to the divine will. All true Christians are conscious that, it is so with them, and this is a great part of salvation. Indeed, it is destruction to be alienated from God, and it is salvation to be reconciled to him. It is destruction to anyone to be a lover of sin. The man who loves evil is a destroyed man, a man who is broken in pieces; that which should be the glory of his manhood is absent from him. But when he is brought to love God, the ruins are rebuilt; and though, as yet, every part of the renovated building may not be finished, the divine Architect, who drew the plan of it from eternity, will never leave the work till the last, stroke of the sacred hammer and chisel shall have been given, and the completed structure shall have had the headstone placed upon it amid shoutings of "Grace, grace unto it." Blessed be God that we have this salvation now, in that we are saved from our former alienation of heart from God.

In the next place, we have received the salvation of our souls in the sense that we are saved from the killing power of sin. Before we believed in Jesus, we were not capable of those sacred actions which are now our daily delight. We could not pray. We may have "said our prayers," as so many do, but, the living breath of true God-inspired prayer was not in us. How could it be in us while we were still dead in trespasses and sins? We could not believe. How could we do so, when we had not received the gift of faith from the ever-blessed Spirit? The fact is, we were under a terrible bondage; and just as a corpse, is under bandage to death, and cannot stir hand or foot, lip or eye, so were we under bondage to sin and Satan. But we are under that deadly bondage no longer; for we are living men, and free men in Christ Jesus our Lord, who has overcome that death for us.

Now we can pray; now we can praise—not always as we would like to do so; but, still, the aspiration is there, and the power is there, and when God graciously helps us by his Holy Spirit, we rise to a high degree of vigor in both those sacred exercises. So, when the killing power of sin is gone, what a mercy it is, what bliss it is; and in this sense also, we receive the salvation of our souls.

More than that, beloved, the reigning power of sin has now gone from every believer. Once, we were slaves to sin, under sin's domination;

sin said to us, "Go," and we went, or sin said to us "Stay! Obey not God;" and we stayed, and at sin's bidding disobeyed God; but, now, sin no longer hath dominion over us; for we are not under the law, but under grace; and though we even now sometimes hear sins mandate, and the flesh inclines us to yield obedience to it, there is a blessed spirit of rebellion against sin within our heart, so that we will not obey sin's commands, but seek after that which is just and holy and right in the sight of God.

Now I am going to take another step, and possibly some of the feebler folk among us may think it is too long a step for them to take; yet I pray God that many of us may practically prove that we have taken it. Beloved brethren, and sisters in Christ, it is possible, and it ought to be the general rule, for Christians to enjoy present salvation, in the sense of being now free, to a very high degree, from sin in their daily life and conduct: nay, more, they ought not to be satisfied without aspiring to be absolutely free from it. It is after this that they should seek, even though they do not attain to it. I am fully persuaded the perfection in the flesh is not attainable here; yet that truth, as I believe it is, has been used by a great many persons as a sort of damper to the sad ambition of renewed spirits. I do not think it ought to be so used, nor that it would legitimately be so used. Suppose I am a sculptor, if it be not possible for me to attain to the perfection of Praxiteles or Phidias, yet I must come as real to them, as I can and I shall not be a master of the sculptor's art unless I seek to imitate those who have been the most proficient in it. Suppose also that through the infirmity of the flesh, I shall never in this life be perfect, like Christ, yet I must have no lower model, nor must I say to myself, "I cannot imitate that perfect model;" but, crying to the Strong One for strength, I must, believe that the omnipotence of God can overcome every sin, and also believe that it is possible for me, by the grace of God, to get every sin beneath my foes; and I must never say to any one sin, "I shall have to spare you, for you are too strong for God to slay." It would be blasphemy to talk like that.

I fear that some brethren think that a quick temper can never be overcome; but, brethren, it must be overcome. The reason why so many professors so often fall into that sin is that they do not believe that it is conquerable, and therefore they do not pray it down. Another person, perhaps, has a sluggish disposition, and he thinks, "I must always be so; it is my nature, and the flesh is weak." It is true that the flesh is weak, but it is equally true that God is almighty; and it is not our own strength but divine strength that is to procure the deliverance of our soul from sluggishness, so we must cry mightily unto the Lord for grace to overcome this or any other sin; to which we are peculiarly prone.

God has not put us into Canaan, and said to us, "You may spare some of those Amorites, and Perizzites, and Canaanites, and Hittites, and Girgashites, and Hivites, and Jebusites;" but his command to us is, "Slay them all, let not one of them escape." There must be no sin tolerated in any believer in Christ; and though you are not perfect, you must never say, "Up to this point, I am perfect; and that is as far as God can make me perfect."

Dear Friends, do you believe in an infinitely powerful God? Do you believe that the Holy Spirit is able to work in you: anything and everything that he wills to work? Then, brethren, stop not short of the highest point that is attainable by mortal men, and seek to be "holy as God is holy." Alas, some professors of religion are hardly even moral; their pretended Christianity is a stench even in the nostrils of worldlings, for they do not conform to the common rules of ordinary decent society but what true Christians long for, is to possess real holiness, to walk with God as Enoch did, to abide in Christ, to shun every false way, to have— "A heart from sin set free,"—and a conscience tender as the apple of the eye. Oh, that we could all come up to this standard!

And we can: it is possible; this is attainable, by the grace of God, through the effectual working of the Holy Spirit. I again say that I do not think that absolute perfection can be reached here, but I cannot tell how near we can come to it. That I would like to prove by happy personal experience; and I beseech every brother and sister in Christ here to join with me in seeking to know how we may, even now, receive the salvation of our souls from the power of sin.

I am quite sure that there are many Christians who have been completely delivered from sins into which they readily fell in their early days. You know that infants suffer from a great many diseases; all through the period of babyhood, they are liable to various ailments which no longer afflict us who are grown-up men and women. So it is with some Christians; when they have grown in grace to the stature of men in Christ, they do not have the little complaints of babyhood. I do not say that this is true of all professors of Christianity; for, alas, there are many of them who have to be wheeled about in perambulators although they are fifty or sixty years of age. While they were little children, we had to bounce them on our knees, and carry them in our arms, and give them milk for babies, and they still want milk, and still want bouncing, now that they are getting gray—gray-bearded babies! But we went to get them out of that state of babyhood, for there is something far better even on earth, than being spiritually mere babes all our lives. May all of us who are in Christ grow to the stature of men in Christ!

The more of such men any church shall have among her members, she better will it be for her, and the more will God be glorified. Let us who are the Lord's resolve that everything that is to be had of God this side of Heaven, we will have. Let us not be content to get just inside Christ's house, and to sit down there, and say, "Thank God, we are safe; we have got over the threshold," but let us seek to press onward to the chief table of rich refreshment and inner fellowship with Christ, and to know the secret of the Lord which is with them that fear him, that so we may find that "glory begun below" of which Dr. Watts so truly sings,

"The men of grace have found
   Glory begun below;
Celestial fruits on earthly ground
   From faith and hope may grow."

RECEIVING SALVATION

And now, secondly, (and with greater brevity, not professing to dive into the depths of the text, but, merely skimming its surface, as the swallow touches the brook with its wing,) *how do we now receive the salvation of our souls?*

First, it is entirely from Jesus Christ: "Whom having not seen, ye love, in whom, though now ye see him not, yet believing, ye rejoice with joy unspeakable and full of glory; receiving the end of your faith, even the salvation of your souls." Everything of salvation that a believer receives, comes to him out of the one storehouse wherein all fullness abides; that is, in Christ Jesus. Never believe Christian, that you will ever get any grace out of yourself. It is a dreary and useless task to send the bucket down into the dry well of our nature in the hope of drawing up a supply of grace. Oh no, beloved, look away from self, and look alone to Jesus, for from him, and from him only, do we receive the salvation of our souls.

Then note that the channels through which we receive salvation from Christ are first, *faith*: "in whom, though now ye see him not, yet believing, ye rejoice." None of us have seen Christ, we sometimes foolishly wish that we had; but believing in him is better than merely seeing him; for many saw him when he was upon the earth, and yet perished, but no man ever truly believed in him, and then perished. Faith is that eye which savingly sees Christ on the cross, and it is only as we continue to look to him by faith that we receive the present salvation of our souls from sin. You can never kill any sin if you turn your eye away from the cross. There is no stream that can cleanse from inward lusts but the precious blood of Jesus that flowed on Calvary. Whoever has been victorious over any temptation, it may truly be said of him, "He overcame through the blood of the Lamb." So that there is no way of receiving the blessings of a present salvation except through believing in Jesus.

Our text also tells us that another channel of salvation is *love*: "Whom having not seen, ye love." The love of Christ is the great force that enables grace to kill sin. The love of Christ and sin are like the two balances of a pair of scales; if sin goes up in our esteem, our love to Christ is going down; and whenever our love to Christ goes up, sin must go down in the same proportion. With little love to Christ, you will walk unwarily; but with great love to your Lord, you will walk carefully before him, and your practical holiness will become manifest to all around you. Though we have not seen Christ, we love, him; and through that love we receive a further assurance of the salvation of our souls from inward as well as outward sin. This is the precious golden conduit through which the power of divine grace flows freely into our souls. Oh, for more fervent love to Christ!

Then our text stays that we also receive this present assurance of salvation through joy in the Lord: "In whom . . . believing, ye rejoice, with joy unspeakable and full of glory." This joy is a flaming sword like that which the cherubim waved at the gates of the Garden of Eden; it blazes, it cuts, it kills. Once let us really rejoice in Christ, as our Savior, and we become guarded from sin immediately. I believe that many sins are hatched beneath the wings of doubt and fear, but when we get away from those ugly things, and live rejoicing in God, then we say "Down with sin!

We cannot endure to have it in our lives." He who has sweet flowers in his hand flings away evil-smelling weeds, and he who has such a diamond of heaven as "joy unspeakable and full of glory" casts away the pebble-stones of earth with which he was pleased before. He who rejoices with joy unspeakable is not likely to be allured by the paltry joys of earth; they have lost all their former charm to him. Their siren songs have no attraction to his ear, for he has heard the celestial note of the harps of Heaven. What bliss it is to be able, to rejoice in Christ as our Savior, for this guarantees to us the salvation of our souls, not only now, but to all eternity!

Why does the apostle say that we rejoice with joy unspeakable? Is it not, first, because this joy is too great to be told? He is indeed rich who cannot count his wealth; he has so much that he does not know how much he has, and he is indeed full of joy who has so much joy that he cannot tell anyone how much he has. I think also that Peter calls our joy "unspeakable" because, if we were to try to explain or describe it to carnal men, they could not understand us. You cannot explain to a person who has never tasted honey, how sweet it is; neither can you explain to a man who knows not the joy of the Lord how joyous a thing it is. He could not comprehend what your words meant; you would be talking to him in an altogether unknown tongue.

Moreover, brethren, you all know the old proverb, "Still waters run deep." The worldling joy barely covers the stones of his daily sorrow, and therefore it babbles like a shallow brook as it runs along in its narrow bed; but the Christian's joy is broad and deep, and it scarcely makes any sound as it majestically rolls on like some great river on its way to the sea. The Christians joy is unspeakable, because it is unfathomable, even by those who enjoy it; and wherever this joy comes, it has a purifying effect, delivering us from sin, and making us thus receive the salvation of our souls.

This joy is also said to be "full of glory." Now, the joys of this world have no trued glory in them; look at the worldly man who is most joyous and glad, what glory is there about him? Any so-called joy that comes through sin is just the opposite of glorious. The drunkard's joy puts him below the level of beasts; but there is an elevating power about the Christian's joy—the joy of salvation, the joy of adoration, the joy of gratitude, the joy of love to God, the joy of being made like Christ, the joy of expecting his coming; all this is glorious joy, and it is full of glory.

I saw lately a picture representing the Coming Man, the Lord Jesus Christ. It represented him as having in his hand cannons, triumphant arches, flags, kings, emperors, and all the insignia of royalty, and blowing them away as chaff is driven before the wind. Come, Oh thou blessed Coming Man; thou knowest how we need thee! Well, he will come at the right time, and all the glory of this world will fly away just like that when he comes. But our joy is full of a glory which the Coming Man, who is "over all, God blessed forever," will keep on increasing so that it shall be to us the fuller of glory for ever and ever. Such joy, as this glorious joy is, makes us look down upon the world's joys and sin's joys as utterly despicable; and so, by lifting us up above them, it further enables us to receive here and now the salvation of our souls.

AFTER THE RECEIPT OF SALVATION

There was much more that I wanted to say, but my time has almost gone. In the good old Puritan times, they had an hour-glass in the pulpit; and when the sands were running out, the minister was warned that it was time to stop, but he often turned it over again, and went on for another hour. I cannot do that, so I must hasten to a close with the solemn enquiry: *have we received the salvation of our souls; and if so, how far have we gone in the reception of it?*

The first and most vital question for you, my hearers, is this, have you received the salvation of your souls? I know that you have heard about salvation, and many of you know what the Bible says about it; but that is not enough. "I know what salvation means," says one; "I know the way." Then take heed that you do not perish in the light. If two men have to go out in the dark, which, is the one to whom the darkness is the more dense! Why, the one who has been sitting in the light! If you go out of your brilliantly illuminated room, you realize how dark it is outside where there is no light above or below. Take care, you who are sitting in the light today, lest for you there should be "reserved the blackness of darkness forever," because you shut your eyes to the light, and will not receive the salvation of your souls.

"Ah, but!" say some, "we profess to be saved." I am glad to hear that, and I would not even hint that your profession is not sincere, but I would urge you to hint to yourself that there is a possibility that all may not be well with you. Are there not many who think they have received the salvation of their souls, but who have not really done so? In St. Peter's, at Rome, I saw monuments to James III, Charles III, and Henry IX, kings of England; but these potentates were quite unknown to me. Certainly, they never reigned in this land, so the royal names upon their monuments are only a subject for ridicule and scorn.

And you profess and call yourselves Christians, if you really are so, it is well; but if you are not so, I can conceive that, in the next world, there may be spirits that shall say to you, "You professed to be Christians, yet you are in Hell! You sat at the Lord's Table and ate the bread and drank the wine in memory of his death—that death in which you had no saving interest, the atonement that never redeemed you!" Oh nay hearers, may this never be true of any of us; but may God, in his infinite mercy, save us, and so may we really and truly receive, and not merely profess to have received the salvation of our souls! If we have really cast ourselves upon

Christ, though we have not seen him, if we do truly love him; and if we have, to some extent at least, the joy unspeakable and full of glory within our hearts, then indeed we have received the salvation of our souls.

Then comes the other question, how far have we received this salvation? If we had a sacred thermometer given to us in order to measure our spiritual heat, what would our temperature be? Are you, brother, above freezing point? I fear that some here are below zero. Have any of you come up to anything like bloodheat yet? What a wondrous heat of love that must have been when the lifeblood of Jesus flowed from his wounds as he hung upon the cross of Calvary! Oh, that we could always have our religion at such blood-heat. Have we reached that spiritual temperature yet? There have been saints, and there are still saints willing to suffer the loss of all things for Christ's sake.

Nothing has been too hot, too hard, or too heavy for them to endure in his blessed service. They have counted shame and loss to be honor and gain if they might but "glorify God, and enjoy him forever." Have we come anywhere near to them? We do have occasional communion with Christ, but have we abiding fellowship with him? Do we dwell near to Christ? But what about these who have not yet believed in him?

I heard an evangelist say, one night in this Tabernacle, "He that believeth on the Son hath everlasting life. H-A-T-H—that spells *got it*." That is an odd way of spelling, but it is sound divinity. The Lord enable you all to believe in Jesus! Then you will have *got it*, as our friend said; or, as Peter, writing under the inspiration of the Holy Spirit, wrote, "Believing, ye rejoice with joy unspeakable and full of glory: receiving the end of your faith, even the salvation of your souls."

6

Salvation by Faith and the Work of the Spirit[1]

"For we, through the Spirit, wait for the hope of Righteousness by faith" (Galatians 5:5).

I T MAY SEEM REMARKABLE that Paul, who was once the strictest of Pharisees, should become the most ardent champion of the doctrines of Salvation by Grace and Justification by Faith. How large a portion of the New Testament is given up to his writings, and the most prominent subject in all that falls from his pen is Righteousness by faith. Did not the Lord show great Wisdom in selecting as the chief advocate of this Truth of God a man who knew the other side—who had worked diligently under the Law, who had practiced every ceremony, who was a Hebrew of the Hebrews, and had profited above many under the Jews' religion, being more exceedingly zealous of the traditions of the fathers? Paul would know, right well, the bondage of the old system, and having felt its iron enter into his soul, he would more highly prize the liberty with which Christ makes men free!

---

[1] A sermon delivered by C. H. Spurgeon on April 11, 1875 at the Metropolitan Tabernacle, Newington.

He was also a man of great learning; he was at home in every part of the Old Testament, and consequently the quotations which he makes from it are innumerable; he also understood the Rabbinical method of spiritualizing, and used it against his old associates, turning the Old Testament allegories into a battery in defense of New Testament principles! He knew how to take the story, as we have seen, of Hagar and Sarah, and to find in it an argument for the Doctrine which he desired to defend. It was well that a man who had been, in spirit, a Pharisee, and in education equal to the most learned of the Jewish doctors, should be engaged by the Spirit of God to defend the glorious principles of Salvation by Grace!

Moreover, Paul was a man of very powerful mind. Has the Christian Church ever had in her midst a man whose arguments are so keen, so subtle, so profound, and yet so clear? He dives to the very bottom of things, but he never darkens counsel by mysticism. Like the eagle, he soared aloft, and his piercing eyes did not fail him as he gazed on the sun. He was amazed by the Revelations he beheld, but he was not dazzled; he spoke some things hard to be understood, which the foolish have wrested to their destruction, but they had to do his teaching great violence before they could pervert it. His intimate acquaintance with Divine things, and the logical conformation of his mind, combined with an immovable decision of character, and a flaming ardor of soul, made him, in the hands of God, the fittest conceivable instrument for the Divine Purpose. He was wisely chosen and set for the defense of the Gospel.

But why, my Brothers and Sisters, such care in selecting an advocate whose previous education and formation of mind so well enabled him to do battle for the Cause? Why was the choice so carefully made? Why such a display of Divine Wisdom? I reply, because this is the point which, above all others has been, is, and always will be, most assailed by the enemies of our holy religion—Justification by Faith is the Thermopylae of Christianity! It is there that the battle must be decided by hand-to-hand fight! If that narrow pass is once carried by the enemy, then the whole of our bulwarks may be stormed! But as long as that fort is held fast, the rest of the Truths of the Gospel will be maintained. The Lord, therefore, sent this mighty man of valor, this Saul the Benjamite—head and shoulders taller than his fellows, of sound heart, decided purpose, and devout spirit to wage war with the adversaries of Free Grace.

I have said that the Truth of God has always been assailed, and is it not the case? It was the clouding of this Light of God, the almost quenching of it, which occasioned the darkness of the medieval period! It was Luther's clear sight of this Truth, and the astonishing thunders with which he uttered it, which brought about the Reformation!

And though there are other Truths of God of great importance—and we would not depreciate their value for a single moment, yet this one, whenever it has flashed forth with brilliance before the eyes of men, has always been the means of restoring evangelical Doctrines, and at the same time exercising a powerful influence over men's hearts, and bringing much glory to the Savior. Despite this fact, or perhaps because of it, it is still resisted, and at the present day it is opposed as much as ever, for you hear, continually, the remark that the preaching up of Salvation by immediate faith in Christ is very dangerous and opposed to the interests of morality; it is asserted that it cannot be supposed to make men any better, and will only create in them a false confidence. They say it will add to other faults the pride and presumption which grow out of an assured security. We continually hear such observations. The present revival has set all the owls hooting, and you know their note—good works are in peril, and virtue in jeopardy!

However well meant, I believe that at the bottom of these amazing objections you will discover the old Popery of reliance upon good works! Human nature always did kick against Salvation by Grace, alone, and it always will! Even professing Christians raise the same objection, but they word it cautiously; they say that the preaching up of Jesus Christ as saving men immediately upon their believing in Him ignores too much the work of the Holy Spirit, and they affirm that a great deal more ought to be said about the preparation of the heart, the humbling and abasing of the soul, the law work, the inward sense of need, and so on!

There may be some truth in this as seen from a certain point, and I should be disposed to hear such criticisms patiently, but I fear that in not a few instances the remarks are suggested by a measure of departure from the simplicity of the Gospel—the very essence of which lies in the words, "believe and live." There is a danger of meaning, "Salvation by works," while we use the phrase, "the work of the Spirit." Zeal for the inner life may only be a convenient method for covering up pure legalism! I will, therefore, assert it boldly that Salvation by feelings is as unscriptural as Salvation by works—and that Paul did not cry out against those who trusted in works with greater vehemence than he would, now, have called out against any who relied upon their terrors and convictions, or who imagined that their feelings, or their doings may be joined on to the finished work of Christ as a ground of trust. Jesus Christ, alone, is a complete and all-sufficient foundation for faith! It is by believing in Him that men are justified—and in no degree by anything else!

We shall use our text, this morning, with the view of dealing with that class of objections which are founded upon the work of the Holy Spirit. It would be a grievous fault in any preaching if it did not ascribe honor to the Holy Spirit, nor could we too severely rebuke any ministry which ignored His Divine working. But, on the other hand, it is no less a fault to misrepresent the Spirit's work, and set it up in a kind of competition with the work of the Lord Jesus! Faith is not opposed to the Spirit, but is the child of it—"We through the Spirit wait for the hope of Righteousness by faith." Two things I shall try to do—may the Holy

Spirit enable me—for on His mysterious teachings my mind relies for guidance into the Truths of God. First I shall labor to declare the Christian's hope; then, secondly, I shall endeavor to show the relation of that hope to the Holy Spirit.

THE CHRISTIAN'S HOPE

Let me *declare the Christian's hope.* "We, through the Spirit, wait for the hope of Righteousness by faith." Concerning the Christian's hope, let us notice, first, its singularity. The Jews had a hope founded upon their descent. "We have Abraham for our father," they said. "We were free born, we were never in bondage to any man; the temple of the Lord, the temple of the Lord are we." They looked down upon Gentiles as uncircumcised and despised them.

Brethren, we have no such hope! We do not expect to be saved by virtue of our parentage; we cannot boast of fleshly descent from Abraham; neither do we rest upon the fact that we are, some of us, the children of godly parents, and that from generation to generation saintly names occur in our pedigree! That which is born of the flesh *is flesh* and no more, however pure the flesh may be! The children of God are born, not of blood, nor of the will of the flesh, but of God! Carnal descent leaves us heirs of wrath even as others. We have no belief in a pretended Abrahamic Covenant made with the seed of Believers according to the flesh; we have no reliance upon anything that comes to us by the way of the natural birth, for that would make us like that son of the bondwoman who was born after the flesh.

Those who glory in their birth may do so at their leisure—we have no sympathy with their glorying. Our hope is altogether distinct from the hope of the Jew; neither have we any confidence in outward rites and ceremonies. Paul has said, "In Christ Jesus neither circumcision avails anything, nor uncircumcision," and we hold that if you put any other rite in the place of circumcision, the same statement is true. No infant baptism, no immersion, no "mass," no sacrament, no confirmation, no ceremony of any kind can, in any measure or degree, be rested upon as the soul's Righteousness!

What if the rites which we believe that God, Himself, had given were authenticated to us by a voice out of the excellent Glory? On those rites we dare not build, no, not for an instant! No blood of bullocks or of goats after the old Law, and no unbloody sacrifice of the "mass" after the modern legality of Roman Catholicism can we rest upon! The beggarly elements of a visible external religion we have left behind as childish garments, unfit for men in Christ Jesus! No, Brothers and Sisters, we are wide as the poles asunder from all who rest upon outward forms, and ceremonial religiousness! We hope to be saved, not because we attend a place of worship, nor because we have made a profession of religion, but because we have obtained Righteousness by faith! We differ, also, from those who place reliance upon moral virtues and spiritual excellences— and even from those who would have us found our hope upon certain graces supposed to be the works of the Holy Spirit.

Had we been the most courageously honest; had we been the most chastely pure; had we never offended against the law of man in any respect whatever. If we could say with the Apostle, "as touching the law, blameless," and if, like the young man in the Gospel narrative, we could say of the Commandments, "All these things have I kept from my youth up," yet would we count our virtues and obedience to be but dross that we might win Christ and be found in Him, not having our own righteousness which is of the Law, but that which is through the faith of Christ, the Righteousness which is of God by faith!

We dare not hope to be acceptable with God because of anything good that is in us by nature, or may be infused into us by Grace. We are

106

accepted in the Beloved, and apart from Him we look not to be found acceptable! Even what the Holy Spirit works with us does not furnish us with any merit which we can plead, for it is a gift of Grace, and no part of our justifying Righteousness. We rest upon Jesus Christ Crucified, and not upon our faith, our repentance, our prayers, our conquests of sin, our likeness to Christ! Right away from anything that comes from us, or to us, we look to Jesus, who is all our Salvation—the Alpha and Omega, the Author and the Finisher of faith! Our faith is singular, then, because it differs from that of the Jew who boasts in his carnal descent. It differs from that of the religionist, who rests upon outward forms, and that of the self-righteous man who depends upon his own works in whole or in part. These three forms of dependence we renounce from the very depth of our hearts! And any other form of dependence upon anything that can be done by man is equally detestable to us! We know that if we are saved it must be upon quite another ground than that of the merit of works of any sort or kind. "We wait for the hope of Righteousness by faith."

Secondly, consider the specialty of our hope. Taking our text in connection with the 4th verse, were mark that our hope is in Divine Grace alone. According to Paul, any man who tries to be justified by the Law has altogether given up Salvation by Grace—therefore we trust for Righteousness in Christ, alone, and look entirely to the free Mercy of God!

If I ever get to Heaven it will be in no measure because I deserve to be there, but because God willed that I should enter Glory by His abounding Grace! No man has any claim upon God whatever! If God gives man what he may claim in justice, He will award him eternal destruction from the Glory of His Power, for that is all man has a right to—he is an undeserving, ill-deserving, Hell-deserving sinner! If any good thing, therefore, comes to us, it must be entirely on the ground of God's Goodness freely given to the undeserving; it is His Pardon extended to the guilty; it is His infinite Compassion looking upon our misery, and determining to reveal itself in a free gift. It is not to be won by effort; not to be deserved nor purchased, but bestowed solely because He "will have mercy on whom He will have mercy, and He will have compassion on whom He will have compassion." Our hope stands on pure Grace, Sovereign Grace, and Grace unqualified!

God blesses us because He is Good, not because we are! God saves us because He is Gracious, not because He sees any Grace inherent in us! He blesses as according to His great Love with which He loved us even when we were dead in trespasses and sins, and therefore Grace must always be the subject of our praise! We can never endure the preaching of any other confidence, for we know it to be a delusion and a snare!

Thirdly, consider the ground of our hope. A groundless hope is a wretched thing, but our hope has a firm foundation. It is founded upon right, and is called, "the hope of Righteousness by faith." Righteousness is a solid basis for hope; if we had a hope which disturbed or destroyed or diminished the luster of the Righteousness of God, the sooner we were rid of it the better! But we need not detract in any degree from the severity of Divine Justice in order to sustain our hope. We expect to be saved by an act of Justice as well as by a deed of Mercy. A strong expression to use—and we use it advisedly; we reckon that by faith we are saved by a method which as much vindicates the Justice of God as if He had cast us into Hell—a plan by which the Divine Righteousness is manifested, rather than obscured. Observe that our hope is the hope, "of Righteousness"; that is to say, a hope arising out of the fact that we are Righteous, and therefore God will treat us as such.

"Strange hope," says one, "for we are guilty." That we admit with deepest shame, and we disown all reliance upon our own righteousness which we know to be but *filthy rags*. But still, we have a glorious hope based upon the fact that we are, at this moment, actually Righteous before God! By faith we are as Righteous as if we had never sinned! Those eyes which can discern the slightest flaw, gaze upon us and discern our inmost thoughts—but they discover no flaw in our Righteousness! Like burning suns they search us through and through, but our Righteousness endures the search, and comes forth unscathed from the heat of that consuming fire! This day, having believed in Jesus Christ, "there is therefore now no condemnation to us." Moreover, "Being Justified by faith we *have peace* through Jesus Christ our Lord." We have a Righteousness which we dare present before God, for it is perfect! In it there is no omission and no excess; we are Righteous before God, and without fault before His Throne! Bold words, but not bolder than the Apostle used when he said, "Who shall lay anything to the charge of God's Elect? It is God that justifies. Who is he that condemns? It is Christ that died; yes, rather, that is risen again."

Now, Brothers and Sisters, if we have a hope founded upon Righteousness, it is well sustained, for where Justice lends its aid to bless, we are sure that all the other Divine Attributes will co-operate! But is it, indeed, the fact that we are Righteous? According to Holy Scripture it is undoubtedly so! We are not Righteous in ourselves; have we not, with detestation, flung away that thought? But we know that it is written, "To him that works not, but believes on Him that justifies the ungodly, his faith is counted for Righteousness." Even David describes the blessedness of the man unto whom God imputes Righteousness without works, saying, "Blessed are they whose iniquities are forgiven, and whose sins are covered. Blessed is the man to whom the Lord will not impute sin."

When we put our trust in Christ Jesus, His blood cleanses us from all sin! Does Divine Perfection need us to be cleaner than that? Cleansed from all sin! When we trust in Jesus Christ, He is made of God unto us Righteousness—do we require a more perfect and glorious Righteousness? Our Redeemer finished transgression and made an end of sin! What remains of that of which an end is made? What more do we need than everlasting Righteousness? What more does God, Himself, require? Don't you know, Beloved, how the Lord, Himself, has said concerning His Church—"This is the name with which she shall be called, The Lord our Righteousness?"

I said that clothed in the Righteousness of Christ we are as accepted as if we had never sinned. I correct myself—had we never sinned, we could only have stood in the righteousness of man. But this day, by faith, we stand in the Righteousness of God, Himself! The works and the dying of our Lord Jesus Christ make up for us, a wedding dress more glorious than human merit could have spun, even if unfallen Adam had been the spinner!

"With my Surety's vesture on,
Holy as the Holy One!"

Here is the footing of our hope, then, that we are Righteous in the Righteousness of Christ, accepted in the Beloved, complete in Him, and perfect in Christ Jesus. This Righteousness we have not obtained by any process which has occupied a great deal of time, and exhibited our ability, and tried our strength—it is the Righteousness of faith! We have believed, and we are Righteous!

"Strange Doctrine," says one. Not at all! It is the way by which Abraham became Righteous, for it is written, "Abraham believed God and it was counted unto him for Righteousness." Along this path all the ancient saints traveled and sang, "Surely in the Lord Jehovah have we Righteousness and strength." This is the only possible way to Righteousness, and blessed is the man who follows it, and knows that by faith in the great Substitutionary Sacrifice he is Righteous before God!

We will now dwell a minute upon the substance of this hope. Suppose you were all perfectly Righteous—what would you expect from God? You cannot expect more, at any rate, than we do who have the Righteousness of faith. We expect to die triumphantly, glorying in our exalted Head! We expect, as soon as our breath has left our body, to be with Him where He is, that we may behold His Glory! We expect to sit at the right hand of God, even the Father, because Christ is there; we expect to rise again at the blast of the archangel's trumpet, when the Lord, who is our Righteousness, shall descend upon the earth! We expect, then, to be manifested because He will be manifested, for, "it does not yet appear what we shall be, but we know that when He shall appear we shall be like He; for we shall see Him as He is." We expect to share in all the glories of His millennial reign, and when comes the end, and He delivers up the Kingdom to the Father, we expect to be there, and forever in the perfection of bliss and Glory to dwell with Him, always singing, "Worthy is the Lamb" We will never sing, "Worthy am I," but always say, "We have washed our robes and made them white in the blood of the Lamb." We will never claim that our robes were not defiled, or that we cleansed them ourselves! We expect this, and we expect it because we are Righteous! Do you see this? No man has a right to expect a reward if he has not a Righteousness to which it is due—but lo, He who is All in All to us, our Covenant Head, deserves the reward—and He has transferred that reward to us who are members of His body! And so are we one with Him! We wait for the hope of Righteousness by faith!

Once more upon this point; notice the posture which our hope takes up. We are waiting for this hope—waiting. Would it not have been better to have said, "We are working"?

No, it would have spoiled the sense altogether. To complete the foundation of our hope of Righteousness by faith we have nothing more to do except to wait for the reward of what is done! To the garment which covers us we dare not think of adding a single thread. Why should we? To the acceptance in which we stand before God we cannot hope to add a single jewel. Why attempt it? Has not Jesus said, "It is finished?"

As far as justifying Righteousness is concerned, we are as Righteous as we shall be when robed in light! We shall cast our crowns before the Throne of God. We are at rest, waiting in peace. It is true we are working for other reasons and other purposes, but as far as the Righteousness of faith is concerned, we are waiting, not working. Waiting—that is the posture of confidence! We are not hurrying, bustling, and running about in anxiety, but we are at rest, knowing that the reward will come. As the workman, when his six days' work is over, goes up to his master's pay table, and waits for his wages, we believe that the meritorious work by which Heaven is procured for us is all done! And, therefore, we are waiting in the name of Jesus to take the reward which as a matter of justice is due to Him, and has been, by His dying testament, transferred to us!

Waiting implies continuance. The Galatians wanted to be surer than faith could make them, and so they ran off to get circumcised and observed days, weeks, months, and all sorts of carnal ordinances! But the Apostle says, "We, through the Spirit, *wait*." We ask no touch of priests, or charm of magic rites! We are thoroughly furnished in our blessed Lord, and are content to abide in Him. Our faith is not for today and tomorrow only, but for time and eternity! We are rooted and grounded in faith in Christ—

> "All that remains for me
>   Is but to love and sing,
> And wait until the angels come
>   To bear me to their King."

"I thought it was a race," says one, "a combat." Oh, yes, we will tell you about that another time, but that has nothing to do with our Righteousness, nothing to do with the ground of our acceptance before God—and that is what we are speaking about just now. As far as that is concerned, "It is finished," sounded from the tree of Calvary, and that "It is finished," brings the Righteous to perfect peace—and there they sit and wait for the hope of Righteousness by faith! I have said enough upon the first point and must hasten to the second.

FAITH AND THE HOLY SPIRIT

The *relation of this matter to the Holy Spirit.* We may be quite sure that the Doctrine of Salvation by Faith in Jesus Christ cannot be opposed to the work of the Spirit of God, for never, without blasphemy, can we imagine anything like a division in the purposes and works of the sacred Persons of the adorable Trinity. The will of the Father, the will of the Son, and the will of the Spirit must be one! It is a perverse forgetfulness of the Unity of the Godhead to suppose otherwise; that which glorifies Jesus cannot dishonor the Holy Spirit—we may be quite sure of that.

But observe, Brothers and Sisters, it is the Spirit's work to destroy the pride of man. All flesh is grass, and all the goodliness thereof is as the flower of grass. The grass withers because the Spirit of the Lord blows upon it. All the vaunted comeliness of the natural man is to be destroyed by the Holy Spirit—and does not the Doctrine of Righteousness by Faith wither up the glory of man? What can do it more effectually?

I have seen the proud Pharisee leer with a scornful hatred when he has heard this Doctrine. "What?" he cries, "After all I have done for years, am I to come to Christ just as if I had been a thief or a harlot and be saved by charity?" He cannot stand it! He will not have it! Now the Spirit of God designs to stain the pride of all glorying, and to bring into contempt all the excellence of the earth—and this Doctrine is the appropriate instrument for His work, and is, therefore, consistent with the mind of the Spirit.

Another office of the Holy Spirit is to exalt Christ. "He shall glorify Me," said Jesus. And does not this doctrine glorify Jesus, since it makes Him the head and front, the *All-in-All* of a sinner's hope by informing him that nothing but faith in Jesus will save him? Is not this according to the mind of the Spirit? O Beloved, the Holy Spirit is no rival to the Redeemer, but a glorious co-worker, delighting to honor the Son! We know, Beloved that the Spirit of God works under the economy of Grace, only.

The Apostle says, "Received you the Spirit by the works of the Law?" Nobody ever received the Spirit by his own works, or as a matter of merit; since, then, the Spirit only comes to men in connection with the great principle of Grace, and Justification by Faith is the essential doctrine of Grace, it must be perfectly consistent with His mind! And you may be sure of this, poor Sinner, that there is no deep, mysterious operation of the Holy Spirit which can, if rightly understood, stand in conflict with the three Gospel announcements that, "Whoever believes that Jesus is the Christ, is born of God." "Whoever believes in Him is not condemned." "Whoever will let him come and take of the water of life freely." Salvation by Grace through faith and the operations of the Holy Spirit must be consistent!

Carefully note that this Righteousness by faith must be consistent with the work of the Spirit because the faith which brings this Righteousness is never exercised by any but those who are born of the Spirit. The flesh relies upon works; it is a somewhat remarkable circumstance, perhaps, but so it is, that sinful flesh, which is barren of all real excellence, always clings to merit. The natural man persists in the belief that he has something to do, and yet he can do nothing! He grasps with all his might the sword which cuts him; you cannot get him to see that—

"Till to Jesus Christ you cling
By a simple faith,
'Doing' is a deadly thing
'Doing' ends in death."

He finds fault with it; he cannot stand it. Of course he cannot—Ishmael is the bondwoman's son, and has the nature of his mother in him. That which is born of the Spirit instinctively clutches the Promise, even as Isaac did, for Isaac knew that he had no right to the inheritance except according to the Promise, for, according to the flesh, Ishmael was the first born. The new-born life in every man runs instinctively to Grace, and lives by faith! You shall never find simple faith in Jesus exercised by any life except the life that is born of Divine Seed in the new birth. Here, then, simple faith and the Holy Spirit are related, for the new heart which the Spirit creates is the only soil in which faith will grow!

Again, faith for Righteousness is based on the Testimony of the Holy Spirit. My Brothers and Sisters we believe that we are justified by faith in Jesus Christ on the ground that the Spirit, in the Holy Scripture, has borne witness that it is so! The witness which God gave concerning His Son is the basis for our belief! We accept the witness of the Holy Spirit as contained in these pages. The Bible cannot be contrary to the mind of the Spirit because it is inspired by the Spirit! So you may rest certain that faith in Jesus Christ as the ground of Salvation cannot be opposed to the Spirit's work, because that faith is based upon the Spirit's own Testimony concerning Christ! Moreover, simple faith is always the work of the Spirit.

115

No man did ever believe in Jesus Christ for Righteousness unless the Spirit of God led him to it; he can never be brought to it unless the Holy Spirit shall lead him there. Faith is as much the gift of God as Jesus Christ, Himself! Nature never did produce a grain of saving faith, and it never will! When a man has believed, he obtains a great increase to his faith in Jesus by the work of the Spirit. The Spirit never takes a man off from Jesus Christ as he grows in Grace, but He establishes him in his confidence in the Righteousness of Christ. The witness of the Spirit in us is a testimony to the faith that Jesus is the Propitiation for sin. He never leads us to rest upon the work within, but points us always to Jesus. When He works in us mightily, our faith becomes even more simple and childlike. We sink in our own esteem, and rise higher in confidence in Jesus. The Holy Spirit could not be supposed to do this if Salvation by faith were an imperfect matter, or dangerous, or dishonoring to Himself! It is by the Spirit that we continue to exercise faith.

Notice my text. I will quote it emphatically—"We, through the Spirit, wait for the Righteousness by faith." It is not because of any other influence, but the influence of the Spirit that we come to rest—and continue to rest and wait while we rest—for the hope of the Righteousness by faith! The Spirit of God works it all, and therefore He is not in conflict with it. It is that which He plants, waters, fosters, and brings to perfection—and He cannot but love it. Ridiculous, then, absurdly ridiculous, is the attempt to make out that the preaching of Justification by Faith is derogatory to the ministry and Deity of the Holy Spirit!

Let us draw an inference or two before we close. From this subject the inference is that whoever has this hope of Righteousness by faith has the Spirit of God. If your hope, Beloved, is based upon your being Righteous through faith in Jesus Christ, you have been born again, and renewed in heart by the Holy Spirit! Many are puzzled and say, "I wish I knew I had the Spirit." They fancy that the Spirit of God would cause some singular excitement in them—very different from quiet penitence and humble trust! I have even known them suppose that it would cause some very astounding swooning, palpitations, and I know not what besides! The best evidence of your having the Spirit of God is your depending upon Christ as a little child depends upon its mother! Others may bring other evidence to prove that they are born from above—let them bring the evidence, and be thankful that they can bring it. But if you have no other evidence but this, "Jesus Christ is my sole reliance, and on Him do I depend," that is enough! All the rest will follow in due course! He that believes has the Holy Spirit in him; he that believes in Him is not condemned.

Draw a second inference. Wherever there is any other hope, or a hope based upon anything else but this, the Spirit of God is not present. There may be much talk about Him, but the Spirit Himself is not there, for "other foundation can no man lay than that which is laid, even Jesus Christ the Righteous." The Spirit will not bear witness to man's home-born presumptuous hopes! He bears witness only to the finished work of Jesus Christ! If you trust that you have the Spirit, but are building upon sacraments, works, orthodoxies, feelings, or anything but Jesus Christ, you have not the Spirit of God, for the Spirit of God never taught a man to place his house upon such sandy foundations!

Beloved Friend, you may, therefore, answer inquiries about what is within so far as they cause you distress, by turning your eyes to Jesus the Lord, our Righteousness. "Look to Me," says Jesus, "and you will be saved." Look away from self to God's appointed Propitiation! On yonder shameful tree hangs all your trust! Look up to Jesus upon His Father's Throne, for there dwells your hope!

One further thought I want to leave upon every mind. Nothing should make us speak with bated breath when we are lifting up Christ

Crucified before the eyes of sinful men. There is no Doctrine, there is no experience, there is no Decree of the Father, there is no Influence of the Spirit which needs, for a moment, make us hesitate when we are extolling the Lord Jesus as an All-Sufficient Savior for the very chief of sinners! I stand here, this morning, to solemnly assert before God that I have not a shadow of a hope of seeing His face with acceptance except that which lies in the fact that Jesus Christ came into the world to save sinners! In Him I do unfeignedly trust, and in Him alone! What if I have preached the Gospel these 25 years? What if I have brought souls to Jesus, not by the hundreds, but by the thousands through the Divine Blessing? What if I have been the means of founding and fostering works of usefulness on the right hand and on the left?

Truly, if these things were to be gloried in, we might glory before men! But far from it! We ascribe them all to the Lord's Grace, and before His Presence we lie in the dust, for we have no hope because of our works! No, nor a shadow of hope! We have no reliance upon our Graces! No, nor a Spirit of a reliance upon them! Jesus Christ stood in my place! I, a guilty sinner, have taken shelter by faith which He has given me! Beneath His wings I hide myself in Him. There is my hope, and that is the hope of every true Believer here—

> "Not what these hands have done
>   Can save this guilty soul!
> Not what this toiling flesh has borne
>   Can make my spirit whole!

> "Not what I feel or do
>   Can give me peace with God!
> Not all my prayers and sighs, and tears,
>   Can bear my awful load!

> "Your work alone, O Christ,
>   Can ease this weight of sin;
> Your blood alone, O Lamb of God,
>   Can give me peace within!"

Now we preach the same hope to the ungodly! Hear what God's Word says to you! You have broken His Laws, and deserve His Wrath! He might justly sweep you down to Hell, but behold, He addresses you in tones of Divine Grace! You have no claim upon Him; you have no right to expect His Mercy because of anything in you that could move Him to pity. But in the plenitude of His Grace He has set forth Christ to be a Propitiation for your sins. And the Apostle adds, "And not for ours only, but for the sins of the whole world." We preach Jesus Christ unto you this morning, and say in His own Words, "Believe on the Lord Jesus Christ, and you shall be saved." Come to Christ, and trust in Him, and you shall be reconciled to God—

> "Your sins shall vanish quite away,
>   Though black as Hell before.
> Shall be dissolved beneath the sea
>   And shall be found no more!"

Whoever you may be, and in whatever condition of heart you may be—it doesn't matter if you have seven devils in you, or if you are as vile as Lucifer, himself, in rebellion against God—if you believe in the great Atoning Sacrifice, you shall have His instantaneous Pardon and acceptance in the Beloved! Oh, hold not out against such free and boundless Love! "God was in Christ reconciling the world unto Himself, not imputing their trespasses unto them." And, "Whoever believes in Him shall not perish, but have everlasting life." Oh, yield, Man! What are your works but sin and death? What are your boasted performances, your virtues, and your excellences—all rottenness in the sight of the heart-searching God?! Quit your refuges of lies, I pray you! Quit them now, lest the avalanche of Divine Wrath overwhelms both you and your refuges—

"Come, guilty souls, and flee away,
　　Like doves to Jesus' wounds!
This is the accepted Gospel day,
　　Wherein free Grace abounds."

Trust His Son Jesus! It is His command to you! In other words, "Believe on the Lord Jesus Christ, and you shall be saved," for, "he that believes and is baptized shall be saved; but he that believes not shall be damned." God save us, for Christ's sake. Amen.

7

Salvation by Grace[1]

"By Grace you are saved" (Ephesians 2:5).

THE CARDINAL ERROR AGAINST which the Gospel of Christ has to contend is the effect of the tendency of the human heart to rely upon salvation by works. The great antagonist to the Truth of God, as it is in Jesus, is that pride of man which leads him to believe that he can be, at least in part, his own savior. This error is the prolific mother of multitudes of heresies! It is through this falsehood that the pure stream of the Truth of God has been tainted so that, instead of flowing on in one clear pure river, it has been sadly polluted. There have been many who have sought to hinder the flowing of the Water of Life, or to divert the stream from its proper current. Many have tried to mingle the fancies and fallacies of men with the Truth as it is in Jesus, in order, thereby, to make it more palatable to poor, fallen, human nature.

It is my belief that all great reforms in the Church of Christ must have for their basis the declaration of the Doctrine revealed in my text— "By Grace you are saved." The tendency of the Church, like that of the

---

[1] A sermon delivered by C. H. Spurgeon in the summer of 1859 at New Park Street Chapel, Southwark.

world, is to fly away from this Truth which is really the sum and substance of the Gospel. A departure from this Doctrine is, in my opinion, the essence of those many errors which, springing up from time to time, have troubled and divided the Church and marred the beauty of the spouse of Christ.

In all times, whenever this doctrine has been obscured, the Church has become either heretical or Laodicean. She has either held some dangerous and damnable heresy, or she has held only a portion of the Truth and held it with so feeble a grasp that it has lost its ancient power in her hands—so that her enemies have prevailed against her. The mightiest men in all ages of the Church's history—those who have been the means of bringing the greatest good into her midst, and the most usefulness into the world—have been those who, rising up like Samson when called to do valiant deeds on behalf of Israel, have made this the distinguishing characteristic of their ministry—the doctrine of Salvation by Grace in contradistinction of salvation by works.

In Augustine's day, there had been a grievous falling away from the simplicity of the Gospel. And when he arose and preached to the world this glorious Truth of God, there was an influence for good which, I believe, staved off the great Roman Catholic heresy, at least for a time. Had the Church and the world but listened to his voice and accepted his teaching, Catholicism would have been an impossibility! Then later, when Romanism had waxed exceedingly strong, the Lord raised up Martin Luther who taught this as the great central Truth of Christianity, that sinners are justified by faith—not by works. After Luther came another distinguished teacher of the doctrine of Grace—John Calvin, a man far better instructed in the Truth of the Gospel than even Martin Luther was—and he pushed this grand doctrine to its legitimate consequences. Luther had, as it were, undammed the stream of Truth by breaking down the barrier which had kept back the living waters in the great reservoir—but the stream was turbid and carried down with it much that ought to have been left behind. Then Calvin came and cast salt into the waters and purified them, so that they flowed on in a clear, sweet, pure stream to gladden and refresh the Church of God and to quench the thirst of poor parched sinners.

Calvin preached, as his great staple doctrine, the great Truth in my text, "By Grace you are saved." It is common, in these days, to call those ministers who dwell mainly upon this doctrine, "Calvinists." But we do not accept that title without qualification. We are not ashamed of it and we would rather be called "Calvinists" than have any other name except that which is our true one. We hold and assert again and again, that the Truth of God which Calvin preached, the Truth of God which Augustine thundered out with all his might—was the very Truth of God which the Apostle Paul had long before written in his Inspired Epistles and which is most clearly revealed in the discourses of our blessed Lord Himself! We desire to preach the Truth of God, the whole Truth of God and nothing but the Truth of God! We are not the followers of any mere man—we do not derive our Inspiration from Calvin's *Institutes* and *Commentaries*, but from the Word of God itself! Yet we hold the doctrines commonly called, "Calvinism," to be none other than the essential basement doctrines of our holy faith. These were the truths that Whitefield preached and that produced the great revival in his days! And these must be the doctrines to which the Church of God must again return, if the Church of Rome is to be razed to its deep foundations, or souls to be converted in great multitudes, or the Kingdom of Christ to come!

My text relates to the doctrine of Salvation by Grace and, coming to it, I ask you to notice, first, that the Apostle addresses certain people who were saved. Next, I want you to notice the meanings of the term, "Grace," as applied in the Scriptures. And I shall finish with some consolatory and practical inferences.

ALREADY SAVED BY GRACE

In the first place, *the Apostle addresses certain people, to whom he says,* "You are saved." He does not say, "You shall be saved," or, "You hope to be saved." He speaks to them as persons already "saved." Now, there are no people on the face of the earth who can be correctly described as "saved" unless it can also be said of them that they are saved by Grace!

I see two things in this part of my text and, first, the Apostle mentions a present salvation. He speaks not to people who were to be saved when they died, or who hoped to be saved in some future state, but he addresses those who actually were saved—who had salvation, not in prospect, but in present enjoyment—who had passed out of a state of condemnation into that of salvation and who looked upon their salvation as being as sure, as certain, as really theirs as their houses, their lands, or their lives!

A present salvation cannot consistently be preached by any beside those who hold the doctrine that salvation is by Grace. Is there a Roman Catholic, in the whole world, who, in harmony with his own creed, can say that he is saved? No, there is not one! In fact, lying as that creed does, it does not profess to put anyone into a position in which he can say, "I am saved." No, the Roman Church not only postpones salvation to the day of death, but positively beyond it! There was Daniel O'Connell, of whom the Pope said that he was his greatest subject in Europe—yet it is not many years ago that we were informed that he was in "purgatory." It was a hard thing that such a faithful disciple of the Pope should be sent there, yet he was no worse off than the bishops, archbishops and cardinals, for, according to the Romish teaching, they all go to "Purgatory!" Of course, the Pope lets them out after a certain time, but that is all he professes to offer—salvation *after* a future indefinite period—he never pretends to say to anyone, "You are saved now." That would be a lie too gross even for the Pope and priests of Rome to utter! There is no such thing as a present salvation in the whole of the Roman Church.

Nor is this possible under any system except that of salvation by Grace. Bring up the good Dissenters, and the good Churchmen, the men and women who are regular in their attendance on outward ordinances. Whatever the ceremonies of their church may be, they observe them with the most indefatigable industry. They have been "baptized" and confirmed. They have "taken the sacrament," or sat at the communion table—according to the phraseology of their different churches—and they believe that, by their constant attention to the outward observances of worship, they will assuredly be saved! But speak to any one of these people, and ask if he can say, "I know that my sins are forgiven"—he will be astonished at your enquiry, and will reply, "I would not have the presumption to say such a thing!"

Appeal to the very best of them, the most devoted, the most earnest, the most indefatigable of those who are seeking salvation by their own works, and ask if they have obtained eternal life. You cannot find one who has done so—they are all hoping that, through the mercy of God, they may somehow and sometime be saved—but none of them will declare that they are now saved. From those who join us in church fellowship, I frequently hear such remarks as this, "I attended my church every day in the week. I repeated the prayers regularly, but I never found any rest to my soul until I trusted wholly in Christ." From others who attended certain Dissenting places of worship, I have had such expressions as this:

"I went up to the House of God and I heard my minister exhort me to be patient in sickness, to love my God and my neighbor, and I tried to do my best to obey his exhortations, but I never could say that I was a saved man, or use the confident language of the spouse, 'My Beloved is mine, and I am His,' until I learned that salvation is all of Grace and, by His Grace, trusted in the finished work of the Lord Jesus Christ."

No, my dear Friends, under the theory of salvation by works, whatever form it may take—whether it appears in the garb of Catholicism, or hides itself under the veil of Protestantism—it is always substantially the same—a man's own works cannot pretend to offer to him the blessing of a present salvation! Take the Arminian theory, which is the least objectionable of all forms of salvation by works—cut it asunder—and you will find that there is a strong taint of Catholicism even there.

"But," asks someone, "do not Arminians rejoice to say that they are already saved?" Yes, but their assertion is contradicted by the assurance which they will give you directly afterwards, that they may finally perish. Although they are now saved, their safety is something like that of a wrecked mariner who, after being tossed to and fro in a stormy sea, is washed up on a rock, from which he may presently be hurled back into the raging billows! Their safety is not like that of the man who has been carried into the lighthouse, or brought to land in the lifeboat, for they believe that, after all they have experienced, they may be lost. It is not salvation that the Arminian possesses—he is only in a salvable state. His condition is that of a man who, if he continues to repent and believe, shall be saved, but he is not truly saved now—he has not been built upon that sure, certain, solid foundation upon which the true Believer is resting. He cannot sing, with Toplady:

"The terrors of Law, and of God
  With me can have nothing to do!
My Savior's obedience and blood
  Hide all my transgressions from view!

"My name from the palms of His hands
  Eternity will not erase—
Impressed on His heart it remains
  In marks of indelible Grace.

"Yes, I to the end shall endure,
  As sure as the earnest is given—
More happy, but not more secure,
  The glorified spirits in Heaven!"

Such a salvation as that—a present one, enjoyed now in all its fullness, in all its riches, in all its boundless lengths, and breadths, and depths and heights—is not possible under any other system but that of salvation by Grace, and by Grace alone! We, of all men living, who preach the doctrine of Salvation by Grace, can proclaim a present salvation in all its fullness.

In our text we also see that the Apostle speaks of a perfect salvation. We teach that the moment a man believes in Christ, he is not merely put into a salvable state, not half-saved—he is not placed in a position where, if he remains, he will be saved, but concerning which there is a fear that he may fall from it—but that he is *already completely* saved! I verily believe that the saints in Heaven, albeit they have received the crown of salvation, are not, as to its essential reality, more truly saved than the meanest and weakest Believer in Christ who is struggling through floods of temptation here upon earth.

For what is it to be saved? It is to have sin forgiven and to be "accepted in the Beloved." The moment a sinner believes in Jesus, his sins are as much pardoned as they ever will be! They are as fully and as finally blotted out of God's Book of Remembrance as they would be if he should live a thousand years of piety. He is as completely clear, as far as the forgiveness of his sins is concerned, as he will be when he stands at the right hand of the Judge at the Last Great Day.

To be saved, however, includes more than forgiveness of sins—it includes the imputation of the righteousness of Christ and, in this sense, also, the meanest Believer in Him is as much saved as the celestial spirits in the Paradise above. Is the robe of Christ's righteousness spread over the Apostles? So is it, at this hour, around the poorest person on earth who is trusting in Jesus! Are those who sing God's praises before His Throne in Glory clothed in the fair white linen which is the righteousness of the saints? Even so are all Believers here below! Each saint is, as John Kent says,

> "With his spotless vesture on,
>   Holy as the Holy One.
> Covered with Christ's righteousness,
>   God sees no spot in His people!"

"But," asks someone, "are not the saints in Heaven more secure than Believers on earth?" Believers on earth are not secure from temptation, but they are secure from destruction—not from tribulation, but from condemnation! They are not exempt from care, woe and suffering, but they are forever delivered from the wrath of God and the damnation of Hell. Not an angel in Heaven is more certain of the eternal love of God than is the feeblest Believer upon earth! If your soul is committed to the hands of Christ, you can never perish! I speak no more strongly than His own utterances warrant, for Jesus has said, "My sheep hear My voice, and I know them, and they follow Me: and I give unto them eternal life; and they shall never perish." To the woman at the well of Sychar, our Savior said, "Whoever drinks of the water that I shall give him shall never thirst; but the water that I shall give him shall be in him a well of water springing up into everlasting life." We are complete in Him—perfected in all the essentials of salvation!

Now, observe, under no system of doctrine, whatever is perfect salvation in this world contemplated except under that scheme which teaches that we are saved by Grace. Under the plan of salvation proposed by the work-mongers, there is no completeness in any of its aspects. Under the old Mosaic dispensation in which God most clearly revealed Himself as the Judge of His people, all "those sacrifices which they offered year by year continually" could not "make the comers thereunto perfect." There was, "in those sacrifices, a remembrance again made of sins every year." However attentive they might be to all the observances of the Ceremonial Law, their salvation was not perfect. But Christ, "by one offering has perfected forever them that are sanctified" and, therefore, He has "sat down at the right hand of God."

Now if under that noblest form of the Covenant of Works, complete salvation was not to be secured, how is it likely to be attained in any of those corrupt systems in which, while men profess to set aside the old Covenant of Works, they yet expect to find salvation? No man but he who believes the doctrines of Grace talks about being completely saved. Ask the Arminian—the fairest and best specimen, sometimes the best of men, though miserably mistaken as to his beliefs—what can he say?

He tells you that if he perseveres in well-doing, in faith and in repentance, he will be saved. Ask him whether he is completely saved, or whether there is something more yet to be done and he will tell you that there is many a step yet to be taken before he will reach full salvation. He may talk about a finished righteousness, but he does not know how it is attained!

We hold that Believers are complete in Christ even now and that, die whenever they may, they will enter into His Presence as being already perfect in Him. Oh, how sweet it is to enjoy a present salvation, which is, at the same time, a perfect salvation! How grateful should we be that it is presented to us in the Covenant of Grace and that it is revealed to us in those blessed portions of Holy Scripture which tell us of the wonderful Grace of God which He has manifested towards His people! "You are saved." Oh, how sweet are these words! Pause, Beloved, a moment or two, and rejoice over them. "You are saved"—saved now, at this present instant—if you are Believers in the Lord Jesus Christ!

THE MEANING OF "GRACE"

Now we are to notice the meaning of the term "grace," as employed in the Scriptures—"By Grace you are saved."

First, it means that if we are saved, it must be a matter of free favor. There is nothing in us that could ever merit God's esteem, or give Him such delight as to lead Him to bestow upon us the blessings of eternal salvation. If we ask why any individuals are rescued from the ruins of the Fall and enabled to believe in Jesus, the only answer is, "Even so, Father, for so it seemed good in Your sight." Certainly, we were not saved because of our talents, for the most talented often remain unconverted. We were not saved because of our wealth, for most of us have none. We were not saved because of the excellence of our disposition, or the holiness of our character, for, even since our conversion, we cannot think of our best services without shame and confusion of face. If

I look upon the people of God, either in the mass or as individuals, instead of imagining that there was anything in them to cause God to love them, I am compelled to say that there seems to have been far more to move Him to destroy them than to save them! Will not all Believers here confess that they are saved not because of anything good in them, but because of Grace most full, and free, and unconstrained?

Further, we are saved by Grace as a matter of Divine operation. From the first holy desire in the soul, to the last shout of victory in the dying hour, salvation is by the operation of the Almighty. Whatever is not worked in you, by God's Grace, will be an injury, not a blessing, to you.

If any of you have a faith, or a repentance, or any condition of heart or life which is of your own making, get rid of it, for there is nothing good in it! That so-called faith which is not the gift of God is really presumption—and that repentance which is not godly sorrow worked by God in the soul, needs to be repented of! I am sure that all there is of good in any saint must have been put there by the Holy Spirit, for it would not have sprung up of itself. Human hearts will naturally grow weeds, but not those rare exotics, those flowers of Heaven, the Christian Graces! These must be Divinely implanted and nurtured, and grow up entirely by the exercise of that same Omnipotence which raised Christ from the dead!

I will go even further and say that if Divine Grace should carry us every inch of the road to Heaven but one, we would be lost because of that last inch! If, in the edifice of our soul's salvation, there is even one stone left for us to put in its place, unassisted by God's Grace, that building will never be completed! From first to last, all must be of Grace. I agree with the highest doctrinalist upon this point, that there is not, and there cannot be a good thing in the heart of any man if it was not worked there by the Sovereign Grace of God.

"Well, but," says one, "is it not the duty of men to repent and to believe?"

Certainly it is, but I am not speaking of their duty. Their lack of power does not excuse them from obedience to God's command. If a man owed another a thousand pounds, it would be his duty to pay his debt, whether he had the ability or not. And, inasmuch as it is man's duty to repent and to believe, herein is the Glory of God's Grace made manifest, in that He accomplishes, by his Grace, what man could never have done! I can truly say that as far as I have gone in the Divine life, there has been nothing good in me but that which has come from God. Let others give their own testimony—if they have any good thing which they have produced, let them glory in it! But I have nothing whereof to glory and must say to the Lord, "You have worked all my works in me as far as they have been any good, but, as for myself, I would cover my face and cry, 'Unclean, unclean, unclean.' Lord, have mercy upon Your servant!"

CONSOLATORY AND PRACTICAL INFERENCES

Now, to close, I want to draw some *consolatory and practical inferences*.

First, how humble that man ought to be who is saved by Grace! The Arminian says that he can stand or fall according to his own will. Ought he not to be proud? What a fine fellow he is! Sing a Psalm in your own honor, Sir, and when you get to Heaven, take all the glory to yourself! You say that you have done part yourself—you admit that the Lord did a great deal for you, but that your own free will settled the matter. Very well, then, give the glory to yourself—sing your own praises forever and ever! But the true Believer says, "I was as clay in the hands of the potter when the Lord began with me. I was senseless, dead, corrupt, till the Lord took me in hand and quickened and changed me, and made me what I am—and I would go back to what I was before if He did not keep me by

His Grace. But I know that what His Grace has commenced, He will certainly complete, and to Him be all the Glory!"

Next, if we are saved by Grace, we, of all people, should have compassion on those who are out of the way. If we are on the road to Heaven, we were brought onto it by Grace and, therefore, we ought to be very considerate of those who are not on it. That good man, John Newton, used to say, "A Calvinist who gets angry with the ungodly" is inconsistent with his profession. He knows that no man can receive this doctrine except by the Grace of God—so, if God has not given to these men the Grace to receive this doctrine, rather pray for them than get angry with them—and ask that they may receive the Truth in which your soul delights."

Then, once again, here is a word of comfort. If we are saved—are saved, mark you—what shall make us sad and unhappy at heart? "Oh!" says one, "I am so poor." Yes, but you are saved! You are a Believer in Christ, so you are saved. "But," says another, "I am so afflicted." Yes, but you are saved. "But," says another, "I am often so neglected and despised." Yes, but you are saved. Oh, what joy would that thought have caused, a little while ago, when the burden of all your sins was upon you! You used to say, "Oh, if I could but be sure that I was saved, I would not mind if I had nothing but a crust of bread and a cup of water! If I could but know that my sins were forgiven, I would not mind being shut up anywhere in the world! If I might know that I was Christ's, the world might say what it liked about me."

Now you do know it, for you are on the Rock and you are saved—so why are you sad? You may now be despised, but, remember, the time is coming when you shall be glorified with Christ! You may be now forgotten by your friends, but your Savior's eyes are on you and your name is on His heart! You are sad, yes, but you are secure! If you believe in Jesus, you may be cast down but you cannot be destroyed! You may be forsaken for a while, but you can never be cast away! Come then—

> "Children of the heavenly King,
>> As you journey, sweetly sing—
> Sing your Savior's worthy praise,
>> Glorious in His works and ways."

Lastly, one word to those who cannot say that they are saved. My dear Friends, there is very much in this text that should cheer and comfort you. The men who are saved are saved by Grace—by God's free favor. There was nothing in them to recommend them to God. You have been confessing, "Oh Lord, I do not feel as I ought to feel." He does not want your feelings as a recommendation. If saved, you are to be saved as a matter of free favor and not as a matter of merit in any sense whatever.

"But," says one, "I cannot repent, I cannot believe." My dear Friend, you are not going to be saved by anything that you can do in your own strength. You need repentance. Do not try to work it for yourself—the Lord will work repentance in you. You need faith. Do not go about to seek faith in yourself—you will never find it there—seek it from Christ. He is the Author as well as the Finisher of faith! "By Grace you are saved." Go and carry this text into every den and sty of pollution in London!

Tell it to the murderer, the thief, the blasphemer, the harlot! Tell it to the man who cannot repent, and cannot pray, and cannot believe! Tell him that salvation is by Grace, and is worked in us by God the Holy Spirit and, as the hymn says—

> "Heaven with the echo shall resound,
> And all the earth shall hear."

Go, then, my Brothers and Sisters, and spread the Doctrine of Salvation by Grace, for this old watchword of the Church is the source of her victory! And when once this shall be her battle-cry, her triumph is sure! The headstone of God's spiritual temple shall be brought forth with shouts, crying, "Grace, Grace unto it."

8

Salvation by Knowing the Truth[1]

"God our Savior; who will have all men to be saved, and to come unto the knowledge of the truth" (1 Timothy 2:3-4).

MAY GOD THE HOLY SPIRIT guide our meditations to the best practical result this evening, that sinners may be saved and saints stirred up to diligence. I do not intend to treat my text controversially. It is like the stone which makes the corner of a building, and it looks towards a different side of the gospel from that which is mostly before us. Two sides of the building of truth meet here. In many a village there is a corner where the idle and the quarrelsome gather together; and theology has such corners. It would be very easy indeed to set ourselves in battle array, and during the next half-hour to carry on a very fierce attack against those who differ from us in opinion upon points which could be raised from this text. I do not see that any good would come of it, and, as we have very little time to spare, and life is short, we had better spend it upon something that may better tend to our

---

[1] A sermon delivered by C. H. Spurgeon in 1879 at the Metropolitan Tabernacle, Newington.

edification. May the good Spirit preserve us from a contentious spirit, and help us really to profit by his word.

It is quite certain that when we read that God will have all men to be saved it does not mean that he wills it with the force of a decree or a divine purpose, for, if he did, then all men would be saved. He willed to make the world, and the world was made: he does not so will the salvation of all men, for we know that all men will not be saved. Terrible as the truth is, yet is it certain from holy writ that there are men who, in consequence of their sin and their rejection of the Savior, will go away into everlasting punishment, where there shall be weeping and wailing and gnashing of teeth. There will at the last be goats upon the left hand as well as sheep on the right, tares to be burned as well as wheat to be garnered, chaff to be blown away as well as corn to be preserved. There will be a dreadful Hell as well as a glorious Heaven, and there is no decree to the contrary.

What then? Shall we try to put another meaning into the text than that which it fairly bears? I think not. You must, most of you, be acquainted with the general method in which our older Calvinistic friends deal with this text. "All men," say they—"that is, some men:" as if the Holy Spirit could not have said "some men" if he had meant some men. "All men," say they; "that is, some of all sorts of men:" as if the Lord could not have said "all sorts of men" if he had meant that. The Holy Spirit by the apostle has written "all men," and unquestionably he means *all men*. I know how to get rid of the force of the "alls" according to that critical method which some time ago was very current, but I do not see how it can be applied here with due regard to truth.

I was reading just now the exposition of a very able doctor who explains the text so as to explain it away; he applies grammatical gunpowder to it, and explodes it by way of expounding it. I thought when I read his exposition that it would have been a very capital comment upon the text if it had read, "Who will not have all men to be saved, nor come to a knowledge of the truth." Had such been the inspired language every remark of the learned doctor would have been exactly in keeping, but as it happens to say, "Who will have all men to be saved," his observations are more than a little out of place.

My love of consistency with my own doctrinal views is not great enough to allow me knowingly to alter a single text of Scripture. I have great respect for orthodoxy, but my reverence for inspiration is far greater. I would sooner a hundred times over appear to be inconsistent with myself than be inconsistent with the Word of God. I never thought it to be any very great crime to seem to be inconsistent with myself; for who am I that I should everlastingly be consistent? But I do think it a great crime to be so inconsistent with the Word of God that I should want to lop away a bough or even a twig from so much as a single tree of the forest of Scripture. God forbid that I should cut or shape, even in the least degree, any divine expression. So runs the text, and so we must read it, "God our Savior; who will have all men to be saved, and to come unto the knowledge of the truth."

Does not the text mean that it is the *wish* of God that men should be saved? The word "wish" gives as much force to the original as it really requires, and the passage should run thus—"whose *wish* it is that all men should be saved and come to a knowledge of the truth." As it is my wish that it should be so, as it is your wish that it might be so, so it is God's wish that *all men* should be saved; for, assuredly, he is not less benevolent than we are.

Then comes the question, "But if he wishes it to be so, why does he not make it so?"

Beloved friend, have you never heard that a fool may ask a question which a wise man cannot answer, and, if that be so, I am sure a wise person, like yourself, can ask me a great many questions which, fool as I am, I am yet not foolish enough to try to answer. Your question is only one form of the great debate of all the ages—"If God is infinitely good and powerful, why does not his power carry out to the full all his beneficence?" It is God's wish that the oppressed should go free, yet there are many oppressed who are not free. It is God's wish that the sick should not suffer. Do you doubt it? Is it not your own wish? And yet the Lord does not work a miracle to heal every sick person. It is God's wish that his creatures should be happy. Do you deny that? He does not interpose by any miraculous agency to make us all happy, and yet it would be wicked to suppose that he does not wish the happiness of all the creatures that he has made. He has an infinite benevolence which, nevertheless, is not in all points worked out by his infinite omnipotence; and if anybody asked me why it is not, I cannot tell. I have never set up to be an explainer of all difficulties, and I have no desire to do so. It is the same old question as that of the black man who once said, "Sare, you say the devil makes sin in the world."

"Yes, the devil makes a deal of sin."

"And you say that God hates sin."

"Yes."

"Then why does not he kill the devil and put an end to it?"

Just so. Why does he not? Ah, my black friend, you will grow white before that question is answered. I cannot tell you why God permits moral evil, neither can the ablest philosopher on earth, nor the highest angel in Heaven.

This is one of those things which we do not need to know. Have you never noticed that some people who are ill and are ordered to take pills are foolish enough to chew them? That is a very nauseous thing to do, though I have done it myself. The right way to take medicine of such a kind is to swallow it at once. In the same way there are some things in the Word of God which are undoubtedly true which must be swallowed at once by an effort of faith, and must not be chewed by perpetual questioning. You will soon have I know not what of doubt and difficulty and bitterness upon your soul if you must need know the unknowable, and have reasons and explanations for the sublime and the mysterious. Let the difficult doctrines go down whole into your very soul, by a grand exercise of confidence in God.

I thank God for a thousand things I cannot understand. When I cannot get to know the reason why, I say to myself, "Why should I know the reason why? Who am I, and what am I, that I should demand explanations of my God?" I am a most unreasonable being when I am most reasonable, and when my judgment is most accurate I dare not trust it. I had rather trust my God. I am a poor silly child at my very best: my Father must know better than I.

An old parable-maker tells us that he shut himself up in his study because he had to work out a difficult problem. His little child came knocking at the door, and he said, "Go away, John: you cannot understand what father is doing; let father alone."

Master Johnny for that very reason felt that he must get in and see what father was doing—a true symbol of our proud intellects; we must pry into forbidden things, and uncover that which is concealed. In a little time upon the sill, outside the window, stood Master Johnny, looking in through the window at his father; and if his father had not with the very tenderest care just taken him away from that very dangerous position, there would have been no Master Johnny left on the face of the earth to exercise his curiosity in dangerous elevations.

Now, God sometimes shuts the door, and says, "My child, it is so: be content to believe."

"But," we foolishly cry. "Lord, why is it so?"

"It is so, my child," he says. "But why, Father, is it so?"

"It is so, my child, believe me."

Then we go speculating, climbing the ladders of reasoning, guessing, speculating, to reach the lofty windows of eternal truth. Once up there we do not know where we are, our heads reel, and we are in all kinds of uncertainty and spiritual peril. If we mind things too high for us we shall run great risks. I do not intend meddling with such lofty matters. There stands the text, and I believe that it is my Father's wish that "*all men* should be saved, and come to the knowledge of the truth."

But I know, also, that he does not *will* it, so that he will save any one of them, unless they believe in his dear Son; for he has told us over and over that he will not. He will not save any man *except* he forsakes his sins, and turns to Him with full purpose of heart: that I also know. And I know, also, that he has a people whom He will save, whom by His eternal love He has chosen, and whom by His eternal power he will deliver. I do not know how that squares with this; that is another of the things I do not know. If I go on telling you of all that I do not know, and of all that I do know, I will warrant you that the things that I do not know will be a hundred to one of the things that I do know. And so we will say no more about the matter, but just go on to the more practical part of the text. God's wish about man's salvation is this—that men should be saved and come to the knowledge of the truth.

Men are saved, and the same men that are saved come to a knowledge of the truth. The two things happen together, and the two facts very much depend upon each other. God's way of saving men is not by leaving them in ignorance. It is by a knowledge of the truth that men are saved; this will make the main body of our discourse, and in closing we shall see how this truth gives instruction to those who wish to be saved, and also to those who desire to save others. May the Holy Spirit make these closing inferences to be practically useful.

KNOWLEDGE OF THE TRUTH SAVES

Here is our proposition: *it is by a knowledge of the truth that men are saved.*

Observe that stress is laid upon the article: it is the truth, and not every truth. Though it is a good thing to know the truth about anything, and we ought not to be satisfied to take up with a falsehood upon any point, yet it is not every truth that will save us. We are not saved by knowing any single theological truth we may choose to think of, for there are some theological truths which are comparatively of inferior value. They are not vital or essential, and a man may know them, and yet may not be saved. It is the truth which saves. Jesus Christ is the Truth: the whole testimony of God about Christ is the truth. The work of the Holy Spirit in the heart is to work in us the truth. The knowledge of the truth is a large knowledge. It is not always so at the first: it may begin with but a little knowledge, but it is a large knowledge when it is further developed, and the soul is fully instructed in the whole range of the truth.

This knowledge of the grand facts which are here called the truth saves men, and we will notice its mode of operation. Very often it begins its work in a man by arousing him, and thus it saves him from carelessness. He did not know anything about the truth which God has revealed, and so he lived like a brute beast. If he had enough to eat and to drink he was satisfied. If he laid by a little money he was delighted. So long as the days passed pretty merrily, and he was free from aches and pains, he was satisfied. He heard about religion, but he thought it did not concern him. He supposed that there were some people who might be the better for thinking about it, but as far as he was concerned, he thought no more about God or godliness than the ox of the stall or the ostrich of the desert.

Well, the truth came to him, and he received a knowledge of it. He knew only a part, and that a very dark and gloomy part of it, but it stirred him out of his carelessness, for he suddenly discovered that he was under the wrath of God. Perhaps he heard a sermon, or read a tract, or had a practical word addressed to him by some Christian friend, and he found out enough to know that "he that believeth not is condemned already, because he hath not believed on the Son of God." That startled him. "God is angry with the wicked every day"—that amazed him. He had not thought of it, perhaps had not known it, but when he did know it, he could rest no longer. Then he came to a knowledge of this further truth, that after death there would be a judgment, that he would rise again, and that, being risen, he would have to stand before the judgment-seat of God to give an account of the things which he had done in the body.

This came home very strikingly to him. Perhaps, also, such a text as this flamed forth before him, "For every idle word that man shall speak he must give an account in the day of judgment." His mind began to foresee that last tremendous day, when on the clouds of Heaven Christ will come and summon quick and dead, to answer at his judgment-seat for the whole of their lives. He did not know that before, but, knowing it, it startled and aroused him.

I have known men, when first they have come to a knowledge of this truth, become unable to sleep. They have started up in the night. They have asked those who were with them to help them to pray. The next day they have been scarcely able to mind their business, for a dreadful sound has been in their ears. They feared lest they should stumble into the grave and into Hell. Thus they were saved from carelessness. They could not go back to be the mere brute beasts they were before. Their eyes had been opened to futurity and eternity. Their spirits had been quickened—at least so much that they could not rest in that doltish, dull, dead carelessness in which they had formerly been found. They were shaken out of their deadly lethargy by a knowledge of the truth.

The truth is useful to a man in another way: it saves him from prejudice. Often when men are awakened to know something about the wrath of God they begin to plunge about to discover divers methods by which they may escape from that wrath. Consulting, first of all, with themselves, they think that, if they can reform—give up their grosser sins, and if they can join with religious people, they will make it all right. And there are some who go and listen to a kind of religious teacher, who says, "You must do good works. You must earn a good character. You must add to all this the ceremonies of our church. You must be particular and precise in receiving blessing only through the appointed channel of the apostolical succession."

Of the aforesaid mystical succession this teacher has the effrontery to assure his dupe that he is a legitimate instrument; and that sacraments received at his hands are means of grace. Under such untruthful notions we have known people who were somewhat aroused sit down again in a false peace. They have done all that they judged right and attended to all that they were told. Suddenly, by God's grace, they come to a knowledge of another truth, and that is that *by the deeds of the law there shall no flesh be justified* in the sight of God. They discover that salvation is not by works of the law or by ceremonies, and that if any man be under the law he is also under the curse. Such a text as the following comes home, "Not of blood, nor of the will of the flesh, nor of the will of man, but of God;" and such another text as this, "Ye must be born again," and then this at the back of it—"that which is born of the flesh is flesh, and that which is born of the Spirit is spirit." When they also find out that there is necessary a righteousness better than their own—a perfect righteousness to justify them before God, and when they discover that they must be made new creatures in Christ Jesus, or else they must utterly perish, then they are saved from false confidences, saved from crying, "Peace, peace," when there is no peace.

It is a grand thing when a knowledge of the truth stops us from trusting in a lie. I am addressing some who remember when they were saved in that way. What an opening of the eyes it was to you! You had a great prejudice against the gospel of grace and the plan of salvation by faith; but when the Lord took you in hand and made you see your beautiful righteousness to be a moth-eaten mass of rags, and when the gold that you had accumulated suddenly turned into so much brass, cankered, and good for nothing—when you stood stripped naked before God, and the poor cobwebs of ceremonies suddenly dropped from off you, oh, then the Lord was working his salvation in your soul, and you were being saved from false confidences by a knowledge of the truth.

Moreover, it often happens that a knowledge of the truth stands a man in good stead for another purpose; it saves him from despair. Unable to be careless, and unable to find comfort in false confidences, some poor agitated minds are driven into a wide and stormy sea without rudder or compass, with nothing but wreck before them. "There is no hope for me," says the man. "I perceive I cannot save myself. I see that I am lost. I am dead in trespasses and sins, and cannot stir hand or foot. Surely now I may as well go on in sin, and even multiply my transgressions. The gate of mercy is shut against me; what is the use of fear where there is no room for hope?" At such a time, if the Lord leads the man to a knowledge of the truth, he perceives that though his sins be as scarlet they shalt be as wool, and though they be red like crimson they shall be as white as snow. That precious doctrine of substitution comes in—that Christ stood in the stead of the sinner, that the transgression of his people was laid upon him, and that God, by thus avenging sin in the person of his dear Son, and honoring his law by the suffering of the

Savior, is now able to declare pardon to the penitent and grace to the believing.

Now, when the soul comes to know that sin is put away by the atoning blood; when the heart discovers that it is not our life that saves us, but the life of God that comes to dwell in us; that we are not to be regenerated by our own actions, but are regenerated by the Holy Spirit who comes to us through the precious death of Jesus, then despair flies away, and the soul cries exultingly, "There is hope. There is hope. Christ died for sinners: why should I not have a part in that precious death?" He came like a physician to heal the sick: why should he not heal me? Now I perceive that he does not want my goodness, but my badness; he does not need my righteousness, but my unrighteousness: for he came to save the ungodly and to redeem his people from their sins. I say, when the heart comes to a knowledge of this truth, then it is saved from despair; and this is no small part of the salvation of Jesus Christ.

A saving knowledge of the truth, to take another line of things, works in this way. A knowledge of the truth shows a man his personal need of being saved. Oh you that are not saved, and who dream you do not need to be, you only require to know the truth, and you will perceive that you must he saved or lost forever.

A knowledge of the truth reveals the atonement by which we are saved: a knowledge of the truth shows us what that faith is by which the atonement becomes available for us: a knowledge of the truth teaches us that faith is the simple act of trusting, that it is not an action of which man may boast; it is not an action of the nature of a work, so as to be a fruit of the law; but faith is a self-denying grace which finds all its strength in him upon whom it lives, and lays all its honor upon him. Faith is not self in action but self-forsaken, self-abhorred, self-put away that the soul may trust in Christ, and trust in Christ alone.

There are persons now present who are puzzled about what faith is. We have tried to explain it a great many times to you, but we have explained it so that you did not understand it any the better; and yet the same explanation has savingly instructed others. May God the Holy Spirit open your understandings that you may practically know what faith is, and at once exercise it. I suppose that it is a very hard thing to understand because it is so plain. When a man wishes the way of salvation to be difficult he naturally kicks at it because it is easy; and, when his pride wants it to be hard to be understood, he is pretty sure to say that he does not understand it because it is so plain. Do not you know that the unlettered often receive Christ when philosophers refuse him, and that he who has not called ninny of the great, and many of the mighty, has chosen poor, foolish, and despised things?

That is because poor foolish men, you know, are willing to believe a plain thing, but men wise in their own conceits desire to be, if they can, a little confounded and puzzled that they may please themselves with the idea that their own superior intellect has made a discovery; and, because the way of salvation is just so easy that almost an idiot boy may lay hold of it, therefore, they pretend that they do not understand it.

Some people cannot see a thing because it is too high up; but there are others who cannot see it because it is too low down. Now, it so happens that the way of salvation by faith is so simple that it seems beneath the dignity of exceedingly clever men. May God bring them to a knowledge of this truth: may they see that they cannot be saved except by giving up all idea of saving themselves; that they cannot be saved except they step right into Christ, for, until they get to the end of the creature, they will never get to the beginning of the Creator. Till they empty out their pockets of every moldy crust, and have not a crumb left; they cannot come and take the rich mercy which is stored up in Christ Jesus for every empty, needy sinner. May the Lord be pleased to give you that knowledge of the truth!

When a man comes in very deed to a knowledge of the truth about faith in Christ, he trusts Christ, and he is there and then saved from the guilt of sin; and he begins to be saved altogether from sin. God cuts the root of the power of sin that very day; but yet it has such life within itself that at the scent of water it will bud again. Sin in our members struggles to live. It has as many lives as a cat: there is no killing it. Now, when we come to a knowledge of the truth, we begin to learn how sin is to be killed in us—how the same Christ that justifies, sanctifies, and works in us according to his working who worketh in us mightily, that we may he conformed to the image of Christ, and made meet to dwell with perfect saints above.

Beloved, many of you that are saved from the guilt of sin, have a very hard struggle with the power of sin, and have much more conflict, perhaps, than you need to have, because you have not come to a knowledge of all the truth about indwelling sin. I, therefore, beg you to study much the Word of God upon that point, and especially to see the adaptation of Christ to rule over your nature, and to conquer all your corrupt desires, and learn how by faith to bring each sin before him that, like Agag, it may be hewed in pieces before his eyes. You will never overcome sin except by the blood of the Lamb. There is no sanctification except by faith. The same instrument which destroys sin as to its guilt must slay sin as to its power. "They overcame by the blood of the Lamb," and so must you. Learn this truth well, so shall you find salvation wrought in you from day to day.

Now, I think I hear somebody say, "I think I know all about this." Yes, you may think you know it, and may not know anything at all about it. "Oh, but," says one, "I do know it. I learned the 'Assembly's

Catechism' when I was a child. I have read the Bible ever since, and I am well acquainted with all the commonplaces of orthodoxy."

That may be, dear Friend, and yet you may not know the truth. I have heard of a man who knew how to swim, but, as he had never been in the water, I do not think much of his knowledge of swimming: in fact, he did not really know the art. I have heard of a botanist who understood all about flowers, but as he lived in London, and scarcely ever saw above one poor withered thing in a flowerpot, I do not think much of his botany. I have heard of a man who was a very great astronomer, but he had not a telescope, and I never thought much of his astronomy. So there are many persons who think they know and yet do not know because they have never had any personal acquaintance with the thing. A mere notional knowledge or a dry doctrinal knowledge is of no avail. We must know the truth in a very different way from that.

How are we to know it, then? Well, we are to know it, first, by a believing knowledge. You do not know a thing unless you believe it to be really so. If you doubt it, you do not know it. If you say, "I really am not sure it is true," then you cannot say that you know it. That which the Lord has revealed in Holy Scripture you must devoutly believe to be true. In addition to this, your knowledge, if it becomes believing knowledge, must be personal knowledge—a persuasion that it is true in reference to yourself. It is true about your neighbor, about your brother, but you must believe it about yourself, or your knowledge is vain. For instance, you must know that you are lost—that you are in danger of eternal destruction from the presence of God; that for you there is no hope but in Christ; that for you there is hope if you rest in Christ; that resting in Christ you are saved.

Yes, *you.*

You must know that because you have trusted in Christ you are saved, and that now you are free from condemnation, and that now in you the new life has begun, which will fight against the old life of sin, until it overcome, and you, even you, are safely landed on the golden shore. There must be a personal appropriation of what you believe to be true. That is the kind of knowledge which saves the soul.

But this must be a powerful knowledge, by which I mean that it must operate in and upon your mind. A man is told that his house is on fire. I will suppose that standing here I held up a telegram, and said, "My friend, is your name so-and-so?"

"Yes."

"Well, your house is on fire."

He knows the fact, does he not? Yes, but he sits quite still. Now, my impression is about that good brother, that he does not know, for he does not believe it. He cannot believe it, surely he may believe that somebody's house is on fire, but not his own. If it is his house which is burning, and he knows it, what does he do? Why he gets up and goes off to see what he can do towards saving his goods. That is the kind of knowledge which saves the soul—when a man knows the truth about himself, and, therefore, his whole nature is moved and affected by the knowledge.

Do I know that I am in danger of hell fire? And am I in my senses? Then I shall never rest till I have escaped from that danger. Do I know that there is salvation for me in Christ? Then I never shall be content until I have obtained that salvation by the faith to which that salvation is promised: that is to say, if I really am in my senses, and if my sin has not made me beside myself as sin does, for sin works a moral madness upon the mind of man, so that he puts bitter for sweet and sweet for bitter, and dances on the jaws of Hell, and sits down and scoffs at Almighty mercy, despises the precious blood of Christ and will have none of it, although there and there only is his salvation to be found.

This knowledge when it comes really to save the soul is what we call experimental knowledge—knowledge acquired according to the exhortation of the psalmist, "Oh, taste and see that the Lord is good"—acquired by tasting. Now, at this present moment, I, speaking for myself, know that I am originally lost by nature. Do I believe it? Believe it? I am as sure of it as I am of my own existence. I know that I am lost by nature. It would not be possible for anybody to make me doubt that: I have felt it.

How many weary days I spent under the pressure of that knowledge! Does a soldier know that there is such a thing as a cat when he has had a hundred lashes? It would take a deal of argument to make him believe there is not such a thing, or that backs do not smart when they feel the lash. Oh, how my soul smarted under the lash of conscience when I suffered under a sense of sin! Do I know that I could not save myself? Know it? Why, my poor, struggling heart labored this way and that, even as in the very fire with bitter disappointment, for I labored to climb to the stars on a treadwheel, and I was trying and trying and trying with all my might, but never rose an inch higher. I tried to fill a bottomless tub with leaking buckets, and worked on and toiled and slaved, but never accomplished even the beginning of my unhappy task. I know, for I have tried it, that salvation is *not* in man, or in all the feelings, and weepings, and prayers, and Bible readings, and church- goings, and chapel-goings which zeal could crowd together. Nothing whatsoever that man does can avail him towards his own salvation. This I know by sad trial of it, and failure in it.

But I do know that there is real salvation by believing in Christ. Know it? I have never preached to you concerning that subject what I do not know by experience. In a moment, when I believed in Christ I leaped from despair to fullness of delight. Since I have believed in Jesus I have found myself totally new—changed altogether from what I was; and I find now that, in proportion as I trust in Jesus, I love God and try to serve him; but if at any time I begin to trust in myself, I forget my God, and I become selfish and sinful. Just as I keep on being nothing and taking

Christ to be everything, so am I led in the paths of righteousness. I am merely talking of myself, because a man cannot bear witness about other people so thoroughly us he can about himself. I am sure that all of you who have tried my Master can bear the same witness. You have been saved, and you have come to a knowledge of the truth experimentally; and every soul here that would be saved must in the same way believe the truth, appropriate the truth, act upon the truth, and experimentally know the truth, which is summed up in few words: "Man lost; Christ his Savior. Man nothing; God all in all. The heart depraved; the Spirit working the new life by faith." The Lord grant that these truths may come home to your hearts with power.

PRACTICAL ADVICE FOR THOSE SEEKING SALVATION

I am now going to draw two inferences which are to be practical. The first one is this: in regard *to you that are seeking salvation*. Does not the text show you that it is very possible that the reason why you have not found salvation is because you do not know the truth? Hence, I do most earnestly entreat the many of you young people who cannot get rest to be very diligent searchers of your Bibles.

The first thing and the main thing is to believe in the Lord Jesus Christ, but if you say, "I do not understand it," or "I cannot believe," or if there be any such doubt rising in your mind, then it may be because you have not gained complete knowledge of the truth. It is very possible that somebody will say to you, "Believe, believe, believe." I would say the same to you, but I should like you to act upon the common-sense principle of knowing what is to be believed and in whom you are to believe.

I explained this to one who came to me a few evenings ago. She said that she could not believe. "Well," I said, "now suppose as you sit in that chair I say to you, 'Young friend, I cannot believe in you': you would say to me, 'I think you should.' Suppose I then replied, 'I wish I could.' What would you bid me do? Should I sit still and look at you till I said, 'I think I can believe in you'? That would be ridiculous. No, I should go and enquire, 'Who is this young person? What kind of character does she bear? What are her connections?' And when I knew all about you, then I have no doubt that I should say, 'I have made examination into this young woman's character, and I cannot help believing in her.' "

Now, it is just so with Jesus Christ. If you say, "I cannot believe in him," read those four blessed testimonies of Matthew, Mark, Luke, and John, and especially linger much over those parts where they tell you of his death. Do you know that many, while they have been sitting, as it were, at the foot of the cross, viewing the Son of God dying for men, have cried out, "I cannot help believing. I cannot help believing. When I see my sin, it seems too great; but when I see my Savior my iniquity vanishes away." I think I have put it to you sometimes like this: if you take a ride through London, from end to end, it will take you many days to get an idea of its vastness; for probably none of us know the size of London. After your long ride of inspection you will say,

> "I wonder how those people can all be fed. I cannot make it out. Where does all the bread come from, and all the butter, and all the cheese, and all the meat, and everything else? Why, these people will be starved. It is not possible that Lebanon with all its beasts, and the vast plains of Europe and America should ever supply food sufficient for all this multitude."

That is your feeling. And then, tomorrow morning you get up, and you go to Covent Garden, you go to the great meat-markets, and to other sources of supply, and when you come home you say, "I feel quite different now, for now I cannot make out where all the people come from to eat all this provision: I never saw such store of food in all my life. Why, if there were two Londons, surely there is enough here to feed them."

Just so—when you think about your sins and your wants you get saying, "How can I be saved?" Now, turn your thoughts the other way; think that Christ is the Son of God: think of what the merit must be of the Incarnate God hearing human guilt; and instead of saying, "My sin is too great," you will almost think the atoning sacrifice too great. Therefore, I do urge you to try and know more of Christ; and I am only giving you the advice of Isaiah, "Incline your ear, and come unto me; hear, and your soul shall live." Know, hear, read, and believe more about these precious things, always with this wish—"I am not hearing for hearing's sake, and I am not wishing to know for knowing's sake, but I am wanting to hear and to know that I may be saved."

I want you to be like the woman that lost her piece of silver. She did not light a candle and then say, "Bravo, I have lit a candle, this is enough." She did not take her broom and then sit down content, crying, "What a splendid broom." When she raised a dust she did not exclaim, "What a dust I am making! I am surely making progress now." Some poor sinners, when they have been seeking, get into a dust of soul-trouble, and think it to be a comfortable sign. No, I'll warrant you, the woman wanted her silver coin; she did not mind the broom, or the dust, or the candle; she looked for the silver. So it must be with you. Never content yourself with the reading, the hearing, or the feeling. It is Christ you want. It is the precious piece of money that you must find; and you must sweep until you find it. Why, there it is! There is Jesus! Take him! Take him! Believe him now, even now, and you are saved.

DESIRING TO SAVE SINNERS

The last inference is for *you who desire to save sinners*. You must, dear Friends, bring the truth before them when you want to bring them to Jesus Christ. I believe that exciting meetings do good to some. Men are so dead and careless that almost anything is to be tolerated that wakes them up; but for real solid soul-work before God' telling men the truth is the main thing.

What truth?

It is gospel truth, truth about Christ that they want. Tell it in a loving, earnest, affectionate manner, for God wills that they should be saved, not in any other way, but in this way—by a *knowledge of the truth*. He wills that all men should be saved in this way—not by keeping them in ignorance, but by bringing the truth before them. That is God's way of saving them. Have your Bible handy when you are reasoning with a soul. Just say, "Let me call your attention to this passage." It has a wonderful power over a poor staggering soul to point to the Book itself. Say, "Did you notice this promise, my dear friend? And have you seen that passage?" Have the Scriptures handy.

There is a dear Brother of mine here whom God blesses to many souls, and I have seen him talking to some, and turning to the texts very handily. I wondered how he did it so quickly, till I looked in his Bible, and found that he had the choice texts printed on two leaves and inserted into the book, so that he could always open upon them. That is a capital plan, to get the cheering words ready to hand, the very ones that you know have comforted you and have comforted others. It sometimes happens that one single verse of God's word will make the light to break into a soul, when fifty days of reasoning would not do it. I notice that when souls are saved it is by our texts rather than by our sermons. God the Holy Spirit loves to use his own sword. It is God's Word, not man's comment on God's Word, that God usually blesses. Therefore, stick to the quotation of the Scripture itself, and rely upon the truth. If a man could be saved by a lie it would be a lying salvation. Truth alone can work results that are true. Therefore, keep on teaching the truth. God help you to proclaim the precious truth about the bleeding, dying, risen, exalted, coming Savior; and God will bless it.

9

Salvation by Works, A Criminal Doctrine[1]

"I do not frustrate the Grace of God: for if righteousness comes by the Law, then Christ is dead in vain" (Galatians 2:21).

T HE IDEA OF SALVATION BY the merit of our own works is exceedingly insinuating. It matters not how often it is refuted, it asserts itself again and again and when it gains the least foothold it soon makes great advances. Hence Paul, who was determined to show it no quarter, opposed everything which bore its likeness. He was determined not to permit the thin end of the wedge to be introduced into the Church, for well he knew that willing hands would soon be driving it home! Therefore, when Peter sided with the Judaizing party and seemed to favor those who demanded that the Gentiles should be circumcised, our brave Apostle withstood him to his face. He always fought for salvation by Grace through faith and contended strenuously against all thought of righteousness by obedience to the precepts of the ceremonial or the moral Law.

---

[1] A sermon delivered by C. H. Spurgeon on April 18, 1880 at the Metropolitan Tabernacle, Newington.

No one could be more explicit than he upon the doctrine that we are not justified or saved by works in any degree, but solely by the Grace of God. His trumpet gave forth no uncertain sound, but gave forth the clear note—"By Grace are you saved through faith; and that not of yourselves: it is the gift of God." Grace meant Grace with Paul and he could not endure any tampering with the matter, or any frittering away of its meaning. So fascinating is the doctrine of legal righteousness that the only way to deal with it is Paul's way—stamp it out! Cry war to the knife against it! Never yield to it! And remember the Apostle's firmness and how stoutly he held his ground—"To whom," he says, "we gave place by subjection, no, not for an hour."

The error of salvation by works is exceedingly plausible. You will constantly hear it stated as a self-evident truth and vindicated on account of its supposed practical usefulness, while the Gospel doctrine of Salvation by Faith is railed at and accused of evil consequences. It is affirmed that if we preach salvation by good works we shall encourage virtue—and so it might seem in theory—but history proves, by many instances, that as a matter of fact where such doctrine has been preached virtue has become singularly uncommon and that in proportion as the merit of works has been cried up, morality has gone down!

On the other hand, where Justification by Faith has been preached, conversions have followed and purity of life has been produced even in the worst of men. Those who lead godly and gracious lives are ready to confess that the cause of their zeal for holiness lies in their faith in Christ Jesus. Where will you meet with a devout and upright man who glories in his own works? Self-righteousness is natural to our fallen humanity and, therefore, it is the essence of all false religions. Be they what they may, they all agree in seeking salvation by our own deeds. He who worships his idols will torture his body, will fast, will perform long pilgrimages and do or endure anything in order to merit salvation! The Roman Catholic

Church holds up continually before the eyes of its votaries the prize to be earned by self-denial, by penance, by prayers, by sacraments or by some other performances of mankind. Go where you may, the natural religion of fallen man is salvation by his own merits.

An old Divine has well said every man is born a heretic upon this point and he naturally gravitates towards this heresy in one form or another. Self-salvation, either by his personal worthiness, by his repentance or by his resolve is a hope ingrained in human nature and very hard to remove. This foolishness is bound up in the heart of every child and who shall get it out of him? This erroneous idea arises partly from ignorance, for men are ignorant of the Law of God and of what holiness really is. If they knew that even an evil thought is a breach of the Law and that the Law once broken in any point is altogether violated, they would be at once convinced that there can be no righteousness by the Law to those who have already offended against it.

They are also in great ignorance concerning themselves, for those very persons who talk about self-righteousness are, as a rule, openly chargeable with fault. And if not, were they to sit down and really look at their own lives, they would soon perceive, even in their best works, such impurity of motive beforehand, or such pride and self-congratulation afterwards, that they would see the gloss taken off from all their performances and they would be utterly ashamed of them! Nor is it only ignorance which leads men to self-righteousness—they are also deceived by pride. Man cannot endure to be saved on the footing of mercy—he hates to plead guilty and throw himself on the favor of the great King— he cannot stand to be treated as a pauper and blessed as a matter of charity!

He desires to have a finger in his own salvation and claim at least a little credit for it. Proud man will not have Heaven, itself, upon terms of Grace! As long as he can, he sets up one plea or another and holds to his own righteousness as though it were his life. This self-confidence also arises from wicked unbelief, for through his self-conceit, man will not believe God. Nothing is more plainly revealed in Scripture than this—that by the works of the Law shall no man be justified—yet men, in some shape or other, stick to the hope of legal righteousness! They will have it that they must prepare for Grace, or assist mercy, or in some degree deserve eternal life. They prefer their own flattering prejudices to the declaration of the heart-searching God! The Testimony of the Holy Spirit concerning the deceitfulness of the heart is cast aside and the declaration of God that there is none that does good, no, not one, is altogether denied. Is not this a great evil?

Self-righteousness is also much promoted by the almost universal spirit of trifling which is now abroad. Only while men trifle with themselves can they entertain the idea of personal merit before God. He who comes to serious thought and begins to understand the Character of God, before whom the heavens are not pure and the angels are charged with folly—he, I say, that comes to serious thought and beholds a true vision of God, abhors himself in dust and ashes and is forever silenced as to any thought of self-justification! It is because we do not seriously examine our condition that we think ourselves rich and increased in goods. A man may fancy that he is prospering in business and yet he may be going back in the world. If he does not face his books or take stock, he may be living in a fool's paradise, spending largely when on the verge of bankruptcy.

Many think well of themselves because they never think seriously. They do not look below the surface and, therefore, they are deceived by appearances. The most troublesome business for many men is thought—and the last thing they will do is to weigh their actions, or test their motives, or ponder their ways to see whether things are right with them. Self-righteousness, being supported by ignorance, by pride, by unbelief and by the natural superficiality of the human mind, is strongly entrenched and cannot readily be driven out of men. Self-righteousness is evidently evil, for it makes light of sin! It talks of merit in the case of one who has already transgressed and boasts of excellence in reference to a fallen and depraved creature. It prattles of little faults, small failures and slight omissions and so makes sin to be a venial error which may be readily overlooked. Not so faith in God, for though it recognizes pardon, yet that pardon is seen to come in a way which proves sin to be exceedingly sinful.

On the other hand, the doctrine of salvation by works has not a word of comfort in it for the fallen. It gives to the elder son all that his proud heart can claim, but for the prodigal it has no welcome. The Law has no invitation for the sinner, for it knows nothing of mercy. If salvation is by the works of the Law, what must become of the guilty and the fallen and the abandoned? By what hopes can these be recalled? This unmerciful doctrine bars the door of hope and hands over the lost ones to the executioner in order that the proud Pharisee may air his boastful righteousness and thank God that he is not as other men are!

It is the intense selfishness of this doctrine which condemns it as an evil thing. It naturally exalts self. If a man conceives that he will be saved by his own works, he thinks himself something and glories in the dignity of human nature! When he has been attentive to religious exercises he rubs his hands and feels that he deserves well of his Maker—he goes home to repeat his prayers and before he falls asleep he wonders how he can have grown to be so good and so much superior to those around him. When he walks abroad he feels as if he dwelt apart in native excellence, a person much distinguished from "the vulgar herd," a being whom to know is to admire. All the while he considers himself to be very humble and is often amazed at his own condescension. What is this but a most hateful spirit? God, who sees the heart, loathes it! He will accept the humble and the contrite, but He puts far from Him those who glory in themselves.

Indeed, my Brothers and Sisters, what have we to glory in? Is not every boast a lie? What is this self-hood but a peacock feather, fit only for the cap of a fool? May God deliver us from exalting self! And yet, we cannot be delivered from so doing if we hold, in any degree, the doctrine of salvation by our own good works. At this time I desire to shoot at the very heart of that soul-destroying doctrine, while I show you, in the first place, that two great crimes are contained in the idea of self-justification. When I have brought forth that indictment, I shall further endeavor to show that these two great crimes are committed by many and then, thirdly, it will be a delight to assert that the true Believer does not fall into these crimes. May God, the Holy Spirit, help us while meditating upon this important theme.

CRIMES OF SELF-RIGHTEOUSNESS

First, then, *two great crimes are contained in self-righteousness.* These high crimes and misdemeanors are frustrating the Grace of God and making Christ to have died in vain. The first is the frustration of the Grace of God. The word here translated, "frustrate," means to make void, to reject, to refuse, to regard as needless. Now, he that hopes to be saved by his own righteousness rejects the Grace, or free favor, of God! He regards it as useless and in that sense frustrates it.

It is clear, first, that if righteousness comes by the Law, the Grace of God is no longer required. If we can be saved by our own merits, we need justice, but we certainly do not need mercy. If we can keep the Law and claim to be accepted as a matter of debt, it is plain that we need not turn suppliants and crave for mercy. Grace is a superfluity where merit can be proven. A man who can go into court with a clear case and a bold countenance asks not for mercy of the judge and the offer of it would insult him. "Give me justice," he says! "Give me my rights" and he stands up for them as a brave Englishman should do. It is only when a man feels that the law condemns him that he puts in a plea for mercy. Nobody ever dreamed of recommending an innocent man to mercy. I say, then, that the man who believes that by keeping the Law, or by practicing ceremonies, or by undergoing religious performances he can make himself acceptable before God, most decidedly puts the Grace of God on one side as a superfluous thing as far as he is concerned! Is it not clearly so? And is not this a crimson crime—this frustration of the Grace of God? Next, he makes the Grace of God to be at least a secondary thing which is only a lower degree of the same error.

Many think that they are to merit as much as they can by their own exertions and then the Grace of God will make up for the rest. The theory is that we are to keep the Law as far as we can and this imperfect obedience is to stand good—as a sort of compromise—say a shilling in the pound, or fifteen shillings in the pound—according as man judges his own excellence. And then, what is required over and above our own hard-earned money, the Grace of God will supply—in short, the plan is every man is his own savior and Jesus Christ and His Grace just make up for our deficiencies.

Whether men see it or not, this mixture of Law and Grace is most dishonoring to the salvation of Jesus Christ. It makes the Savior's work to be incomplete, though on the Cross He cried, "It is finished." Yes, it even treats it as being utterly ineffectual since it appears to be of no use at all until man's works are added to it. According to this notion, we are redeemed as much by our own doing as by the ransom price of Jesus' blood—man and Christ go shares, both in the work and in the glory! This is an intense form of arrogant treason against the majesty of Divine Mercy! This is a capital crime which will condemn all who continue in it.

May God deliver us from thus insulting the Throne of Grace by bringing a purchase price in our own hands as if we could deserve such peerless gifts of love!

More than that, he who trusts in himself, his feelings, his works, his prayers, or in anything except the Grace of God virtually gives up trusting in the Grace of God altogether! Don't you know that God's Grace will never share the work with man's merit? As oil will not combine with water, so neither will human merit and heavenly mercy mix together! The Apostle says in Romans 11:6, "If by Grace, then it is no more of works: otherwise Grace is no more Grace. But if it is of works, then is it no more Grace: otherwise work is no more work."

You must either have salvation wholly because you deserve it, or wholly because God graciously bestows it, though you do not deserve it! You must receive salvation at the Lord's hands either as a debt or as a charity—there can be no mingling of the ideas. That which is a pure gift of favor cannot also be a reward of personal merit! A combination of the two principles of Law and Grace is utterly impossible. Trusting in our own works in any degree effectually shuts us out from all hope of salvation by Grace—and so it frustrates the Grace of God.

There is another form of this crime, that when men preach up human works, sufferings, feelings, or emotions as the ground of salvation, they deny the sinner confidence in Christ, for as long as a man can maintain any hope in himself, he will never look to the Redeemer. We may preach forever and ever, but as long as there remains latent in any one bosom a hope that he can effectually clear himself from sin and win the favor of God by his own works, that man will never accept the proclamation of free pardon through the blood of Christ! We know that we cannot frustrate the Grace of God—it will have its way and the eternal purpose shall be fulfilled. But as the tendency of all teaching which mixes up works with Grace is to take men away from believing in the Lord Jesus

Christ, its tendency is to frustrate the Grace of God and every act is to be judged by its tendency even if the Lord's Divine power prevents its working out its natural result.

No man can lay another Foundation than that which is laid, but inasmuch as they try to do so they are guilty of despising the Foundation of God as much as those builders of the olden times who rejected the stone which God had chosen to be the head of the corner. May the Grace of God keep us from such a crime as this, lest the blood of other men's souls should crimson our garments. This hoping to be saved by our own righteousness robs God of His Glory. It as good as says, "We do not need Grace. We need no free favor." It reads of the New Covenant, which Infinite Love has made, but by clinging to the Old Covenant it puts dishonor upon it. In its heart it murmurs, "What need of this Covenant of Grace? The Covenant of Works answers every purpose for us."

It reads of the great gift of Grace in the Person of Jesus Christ and it does despite thereto by the secret thought that human works are as good as the life and death of the Son of God! It cries, "We will not have this Man to save us." A self-righteous hope casts a slur upon the Glory of God since it is clear that if a man could be saved by his own works, he would naturally have the honor of it. But if a man is saved by the free Grace of God, then God is glorified. Woe unto those who teach a doctrine which would pluck the royal Crown from the head of our Sovereign Lord and disgrace the Throne of His glory! God help us to be clear of this rank offense against high Heaven. I grow warm upon such a subject as this, for my indignation rises against that which does dishonor to my Lord and frustrates His Grace.

This is a sin so gross that even the heathen cannot commit it! They have never heard of the Grace of God and therefore they cannot put a slight upon it—when they perish it will be with a far lighter doom than those who have been told that God is gracious and ready to pardon and yet turn on their heels and wickedly boast of innocence and pretend to be clean in the sight of God! This is a sin which devils cannot commit. With all the obstinacy of their rebellion, they can never reach to this! They have never had the sweet notes of Free Grace and dying love ringing in their ears and, therefore, they have never refused the heavenly invitation. What has never been presented to their acceptance cannot be the object of their rejection. Thus, my Hearer, if you should fall into this deep ditch, you will sink lower than the heathen, lower than Sodom and Gomorrah and lower than the devil, himself! Wake up, I pray, and do not dare to frustrate the Grace of God! The second great crime which self-justification commits is making Christ to be dead in vain. This is plain enough.

If salvation can be by the works of the Law, why did our Lord Jesus die to save us? Oh, You bleeding Lamb of God, Your Incarnation is a marvel, but Your death upon the accursed tree is such a miracle of mercy as fills all Heaven with astonishment! Will any dare to say that Your death, Oh Incarnate God, was a superfluity, a wanton waste of suffering? Do they dare think You a generous but unwise enthusiast whose death was needless? Can there be any who think Your Cross a vain thing? Yes, thousands virtually do this and, in fact, all do who make it out that men might have been saved in some other way, or may now be saved by their own works and doings! They who say that the death of Christ goes only part of the way and that man must do something in order to merit eternal life—these, I say, make this death of Christ to be only partially effective and, in yet clearer terms, ineffectual in and of itself!

If it is even hinted that the blood of Jesus is not price enough till man adds his silver or his gold, then His blood is not our redemption at all and Christ is no Redeemer! If it is taught that our Lord's bearing of sin for us did not make a perfect Atonement and that it is ineffectual till we either do or suffer something to complete it—then in the supplemental work lies the real virtue and Christ's work, is in itself, insufficient! His death cry of, "It is finished," must have been all a mistake if it is still not finished! And if a believer in Christ is not completely saved by what Christ has done, but must do something, himself, to complete it, then salvation was not finished and the Savior's work remains imperfect till we, poor sinners, lend a hand to make up for His deficiencies! What blasphemy lies in such a supposition that Christ, on Calvary, made a needless and a useless offering of Himself and any man among you can be saved by the works of the Law!

This spirit also rejects the Covenant which was sealed with Christ's death. For if we can be saved by the old Covenant of Works, then the New Covenant was not required. In God's wisdom the New Covenant was brought in because the first had grown old and was void by transgression. But if it is not void, then the New Covenant is an idle innovation and the Sacrifice of Jesus ratified a foolish transaction! I loathe the words while I pronounce them! No one ever was saved under the Covenant of Works nor ever will be—the New Covenant is introduced for that reason—but if there is salvation by the first, then what need was there of the second? Self-righteousness, as far as it can, disannuls the Covenant, breaks its seal and does despite to the blood of Jesus Christ which is the substance, the certificate and the seal of that Covenant.

If you hold that a man can be saved by his own good works, you pour contempt upon the Testament of Love which the death of Jesus has put in force, for there is no need to receive as a legacy of love that which can be earned as the wage of work! Oh dear People, this is a sin against each Person of the sacred Trinity! It is a sin against the Father. How could He be wise and good and yet give His only Son to die on yonder tree in anguish if man's salvation could be worked by some other means? It is a sin against the Son of God—you dare to say that our redemption price could have been paid another way and, therefore, His death was not absolutely necessary for the redemption of the world. Or, if necessary, yet not effectual, for it requires something to be added to it before it can effect its purpose.

It is a sin against the Holy Spirit and beware how you sin against Him, for such sins are fatal! The Holy Spirit bears witness to the glorious perfection and unconquerable power of the Redeemer's work and woe to those who reject that witness! He has come into the world, on purpose, that He may convict men of the sin of not believing in Jesus Christ and, therefore, if we think that we can be saved apart from Christ we do despite to the Spirit of His Grace. The doctrine of Salvation by works is a sin against all the fallen sons of Adam, for if men cannot be saved except by their own works, what hope is left for any transgressor? You shut the gates of Mercy on mankind! You condemn the guilty to die without the possibility of remission! You deny all hope of welcome to the returning prodigal, all prospect of Paradise to the dying thief! If Heaven is by works, thousands of us will never see its gates. I know that I never shall. You fine fellows may rejoice in your prospects, but what is to become of us? You ruin us all by your boastful scheme!

Nor is this all. It is a sin against the saints, for none of them have any other hope except in the blood and righteousness of Jesus Christ. Remove the doctrine of the atoning blood and you have taken all away! Our foundation is gone! If you speak thus you offend the whole generation of godly men. I go further—work-mongering is a sin against the perfect ones above! The doctrine of salvation by works would silence the hallelujahs of Heaven. Hush, you choristers, what meaning is there in your song? You are chanting, "Unto Him that loved us and washed us from our sins in His own blood."

But why do you sing so? If salvation is by works, your ascriptions of praise are empty flatteries. You ought to sing, "Unto ourselves who kept our garments clean, to us be glory forever and ever!" Or at least, "unto ourselves whose acts made the Redeemer's work effectual be a full share of praise."

But a self-lauding note was never heard in Heaven and, therefore, we feel sure that the doctrine of self-justification is not of God. I charge you—renounce it as the foe of God and man! This proud system is a sin of deepest dye against my Master, Jesus Christ! I cannot endure to think of the insult which it puts upon our dying Lord! If you have made Christ to live in vain, that is bad enough, but to represent Him as having died in vain? What shall be said of this? That Christ came to earth for nothing is a most horrible statement, but that He became obedient to the death of the Cross without result is profanity at its worst!

SELF-JUSTIFICATION AFFLICTS MANY

I will say no more concerning the nature of these sins, but in the second place proceed to the solemn fact that *these two great crimes are committed by many people.* I am afraid they are committed by some who hear me this day. Let everyone search himself and see if these accursed things are not hidden in his heart and if they are, let him cry unto God for deliverance from them! Assuredly these crimes are chargeable on those who trifle with the Gospel! Here is the greatest discovery that was ever made—the most wonderful piece of knowledge that ever was revealed and yet you do not think it worth a thought! You come now and then to hear a sermon, but you hear without heart. You read the Scriptures occasionally, but you do not search them as for hidden treasure.

It is not your first objective in life to thoroughly understand and heartily to receive the Gospel which God has proclaimed—yet such ought to be the case. What, my Friend? Does your indifference say that the

Grace of God is of no great value in your esteem? You do not think it worth the trouble of prayer, of Bible-reading and attention? The death of Christ is nothing to you—a very beautiful fact, no doubt—you know the story well, but you do not care enough about it to wish to be a partaker in its benefits? His blood may have power to cleanse from sin, but you do not need remission? His death may be the life of men, but you do not long to live by Him? To be saved by the atoning blood does not strike you as being half as important as to carry on your business at a profit and acquire a fortune for your family? By thus trifling with these precious things, you do, as far as you can, frustrate the Grace of God and make Christ to die in vain!

Another set of people who do this are those who have no sense of guilt. Perhaps they are naturally amiable, civil, honest and generous people and they think that these natural virtues are all that is needed. We have many such in whom there is much that is lovely, but the one thing necessary is lacking—they are not conscious that they ever did anything very wrong! They think themselves certainly as good as others and in some respects rather *better*. It is highly probable that you are as good as others and even better than others, but still, do you not see, my dear Friend, if I am addressing one such person, that if you are so good that you are to be saved by your goodness, you put the Grace of God out of court and make it vain? The whole have no need of the Physician—only they that are sick require His skill and, therefore, it was needless that Christ should die for such as you because you, in your own opinion, have done nothing worthy of death.

You claim that you have done nothing very bad and yet there is one thing in which you have grievously transgressed and I beg you not to be angry when I charge you with it. You are very bad because you are so proud as to think yourself righteous, though God has said that there is none righteous, no, not one! You tell your God that He is a liar! His

Word accuses you and His Law condemns you but you will not believe Him and actually boast of having a righteousness of your own!

This is high presumption and arrogant pride and may the Lord purge you from it! Will you lay this to heart and remember that if you have never been guilty of anything else, this is sin enough to make you mourn before the Lord day and night? You have, as far as you could, by your proud opinion of yourself made void the Grace of God and declared that Christ died in vain. Hide your face for shame and entreat for mercy for this glaring offense!

Another sort of people may fancy that they shall escape but we must now come home to them. Those who despair will often cry, "I know I cannot be saved except by Grace, for I am such a great sinner! But, alas, I am too great a sinner to be saved at all! I am too black for Christ to wash out my sins." Ah, my dear Friend, though you know it not, you are making void the Grace of God by denying its power and limiting its might! You doubt the efficacy of the Redeemer's blood and the power of the Father's Grace. What? The Grace of God not able to save? Is not the Father of our Lord Jesus able to forgive sin? We joyfully sing—

> "Who is a pardoning God like Thee?
> Or who has Grace so rich and free?"

And you dare say He cannot forgive you and this in the teeth of His many promises of mercy? He says, "All manner of sin and of blasphemy shall be forgiven unto men." And, "Come now and let us reason together, says the Lord: though your sins are as scarlet, they shall be as white as snow; though they are red like crimson, they shall be as wool."

You say that this is not true! Thus you frustrate the Grace of God and you make out that Christ died in vain, at least for you, for you say that He cannot cleanse you. Oh do not say this! Let not your unbelief give the lie to God. Oh, believe that He is able to save even you and freely, at this very moment, and put all your sin away and to accept you in Christ Jesus! Take heed of despondency, for if you do not trust Him, you will make void His Grace. And those, I think, commit this sin in a large measure, who make a mingle-mangle of the Gospel. I mean this—when we preach the Gospel we have only to say, "Sinners, you are guilty! You never can be anything else but guilty in and of yourselves—if that sin of yours is pardoned, it must be through an act of Sovereign Grace and not because of anything in you, or that can be done by you. Grace must be given to you because Jesus died and for no other reason and the way by which you can have that Grace is simply by trusting Christ. By faith in Jesus Christ you shall obtain full forgiveness." This is pure Gospel.

If the man turns round and enquires, "Why do I have a right to believe in Christ?" If I tell him that he is warranted to believe in Christ because he feels a law-work within, or because he has holy desires, I have made a mess of it. I have put something of the man into the question and marred the glory of Grace. My answer is, "Man, your right to believe in Christ lies not in what you are or feel, but in God's command to you *to believe* and in God's promise which is made to every creature under Heaven that whoever believes in Jesus Christ shall be saved." This is our commission, "Go you into all the world and preach the Gospel to every creature. He that believes and is baptized shall be saved."

If you are a creature, we preach that Gospel to you! Trust Christ and you are saved. Not because you are a sensible sinner, or a penitent sinner, or anything else, but simply because God, of His Free Grace, with no consideration rendered to Him on your part, but *gratis* and for nothing, freely forgives all your debts for the sake of Jesus Christ. Now I have not mangled the Gospel—there it is with nothing of the creature about it but the man's faith and even that is the Holy Spirit's gift! Those who mingle their, "ifs," and, "buts," and insist upon, "you must do this and feel that before you may accept Christ," frustrate the Grace of God, in a measure, and do damage to the glorious Gospel of the blessed God.

And so, once more, to those who apostatize. Do I speak to any here who were once professors of religion—who once used to offer prayer in the assembly—who once walked as saints but now have gone back, breaking the Sabbath, forsaking the house of God and living in sin? You, my Friend, say by your course of life: "I had the Grace of God, but I do not care about it! It is worth nothing. I have rejected it, I have given it up! I have made it void! I have gone back to the world." You do as good as say, "I did once trust in Jesus Christ, but He is not worth trusting."

You have denied Him—you have sold your Lord and Master! I will not now go into the question as to whether you ever were sincere, though I believe you never were. But on your own showing such is your case. Take heed lest these two terrible crimes should rest upon you—that you do frustrate the Grace of God and make Christ to be dead in vain.

NO TRUE BELIEVER WILL BE GUILTY

On my third point I shall carry with me the deep convictions and the joyful confidences of all true Believers. It is this, that *no true believer will be guilty of these crimes.* In his very soul he loathes these infamous sins. First of all, no believer in Christ can bear to think of frustrating of the Grace of God or the making it void. Come, now, honest hearts, I speak to you! Do you trust in Grace alone, or do you, in some measure, rest in yourselves? Do you, even in a small degree, depend upon your own feelings, your own faithfulness, your own repentance? I know you abhor the very thought! You have not even the shadow of a hope nor the semblance of a confidence in anything you ever were, or ever can be, or ever hope to be! You fling this away as a foul rag full of filth which you would hurl out of the universe if you could.

I acknowledge that though I have preached the Gospel with all my heart and glory in it, yet I cast my preaching away as dross and dung if I think of them as a ground of reliance! And though I have brought many souls to Christ, blessed be His name, I never dare, for one moment, to put the slightest confidence in that fact as to my own salvation, for I know that I, after having preached to others, may yet be a castaway. I cannot rest in a successful ministry, or an edified Church, but I repose alone in my Redeemer! What I say of myself I know that each one of you will say for himself. Your almsgivings, your prayers, your tears, your suffering persecution, your gifts to the Church, your earnest work in the Sunday school or elsewhere—did you ever think of putting these side by side with the blood of Christ as your hope?

No, you never dreamed of it! I am sure you never did and the mention of it is utterly loathsome to you, is it not? Grace, Grace, Grace is your only hope. Moreover, you have not only renounced all confidence in works, but you renounce it this day more heartily than ever before. The older you are and the more holy you become, the less do you think of trusting in yourself! The more we grow in Grace the more we grow in love with Grace—the more we search into our hearts and the more we know of the holy Law of God, the deeper is our sense of unworthiness and consequently the higher is our delight in rich, free, unmerited mercy—the free gift of the royal heart of God!

Tell me, does not your heart leap within you when you hear the Doctrines of Grace? I know there are some who never felt themselves to be sinners, who shift about as if they were sitting on thorns when I am preaching Grace and nothing else but Grace—but it is not so with you who are resting in Christ. "Oh, no," you say, "ring that bell again, Sir! Ring that bell again! There is no music like it. Touch that string again, it is our favorite note!" When you get down in spirits and depressed, what sort of book do you like to read? Is it not a Book about the Grace of God?

What do you turn to in the Scriptures? Do you not turn to the promises made to the guilty, the ungodly, the sinner? And do you not find that only in the Grace of God and only at the foot of the Cross is there any rest for you? I know it is so! Then you can rise up and say with Paul, "I do not frustrate the Grace of God. Some may, if they like, but God forbid that I should ever make it void, for it is all my salvation and all my desire."

The true Believer is also free from the second crime—he does not make Christ to be dead in vain. No, no, no! He trusts in the death of Christ! He puts his sole and entire reliance upon the great Substitute who loved and lived and died for him! He does not dare to associate with the bleeding Sacrifice his poor bleeding heart, or his prayers, or his sanctification, or anything else. "None but Christ, none but Christ," is his soul's cry. He detests every proposal to mix anything of ceremony or of legal action with the finished work of Jesus Christ. The longer we live, I trust, dear Brothers and Sisters, the more we see the Glory of God in the face of Jesus Christ! We are struck with admiration at the wisdom of the way by which the Substitute was introduced—that God might smite sin and yet spare the sinner—we are lost in admiration at the matchless love of God, that He spared not His own Son!

We are filled with reverent adoration at the love of Christ, that when He knew the price of pardon was His blood, His pity never withdrew. What is more, we not only joy in Christ, but we feel an increasing oneness with Him. We did not know it at first, but we know it now, that we were crucified with Him, that we were buried with Him, that we rose again with Him! We are not going to have Moses for a ruler, or Aaron for a priest, for Jesus is both King and Priest to us! Christ is in us and we are in Christ and we are complete in Him and nothing can be tolerated as an aid to the blood and righteousness of Jesus Christ our Lord! We are one with Him and being one with Him we realize more, every day, that He did *not* die in vain! His death has bought us real life! His death has already set us free from the bondage of sin and has even now brought us deliverance from the fear of eternal wrath.

His death has bought us eternal life, has bought us sonship and all the blessings that go with it which the Fatherhood of God takes care to bestow! The death of Christ has shut the gates of Hell for us and opened the gates of Heaven! The death of Christ has worked mercies for us—not visionary or imaginary but real and true—which this very day we enjoy and so we are in no danger of thinking that Christ died in vain. It is our joy to hold two great principles which I will leave with you, hoping that you will suck marrow and fatness out of them. These are the two principles: *the Grace of God cannot be frustrated,* and *Jesus Christ died not in vain.* These two principles, I think, lie at the bottom of all sound doctrine. The Grace of God cannot be frustrated! Its eternal purpose will be fulfilled, its Sacrifice and seal shall be effectual—the chosen ones of Grace shall be brought to Glory!

There shall be no failures as to God's plan in any point whatever! At the last, when all shall be summed up, it shall be seen that Grace reigned through righteousness unto eternal life and the top stone shall be brought out with shouts of "Grace, Grace unto it." And as Grace cannot be frustrated, so Christ did not die in vain! Some seem to think that there were purposes in Christ's heart which will never be accomplished. We have not so learned Christ. What He died to do shall be done—those He bought, He will have—those He redeemed shall be free. There shall be no failure of reward for Christ's wondrous work! He shall see of the travail of His soul and shall be satisfied.

On these two principles I throw back my soul to rest. Believing in His Grace that Grace shall never fail me. "My Grace is sufficient for you," says the Lord and so shall it be. Believing in Jesus Christ, His death must save me. It cannot be, oh Calvary, that you should fail! Oh Gethsemane, that your bloody sweat should be in vain. Through Divine Grace, resting in our Savior's precious blood, we must be saved! Joy and rejoice with me and go your way to tell it to others! God bless you in so doing, for Jesus' sake. Amen.

10

Salvation to the Uttermost[1]

"Where He is able also to save them to the uttermost that come unto God by Him, seeing He ever liveth to make intercession for them" (Hebrews 7:25).

SALVATION IS A DOCTRINE peculiar to revelation. Revelation affords us a complete history of it, but nowhere else can we find any trace thereof. God has written many books, but only one book has had for its aim the teaching of the ways of mercy. He has written the great book of creation, which is our duty and our pleasure to read. It is a volume embellished on its surface with starry gems and rainbow colors, and containing in its inner leaves marvels at which the wise may wonder for age, and yet find a fresh theme for their conjectures.

Nature is the spelling-book of man, in which he may learn his Maker's name, he hath studded it with embroidery, with gold, with gems. There are doctrines of truth in the mighty stars, and there are lessons written on the green earth and in the flowers springing up from the ground. We read the books of God when we see the storm and tempest, for all things speak as God would have them; and if our ears are open we

---

[1] A sermon delivered by C. H. Spurgeon on June 6, 1856 at Exeter Hall, Strand.

may hear the voice of God in the rippling of every rill, in the roll of every thunder, in the brightness of every lightning, in the twinkling of every star, in the budding of every flower. God has written the great book of creation, to teach us what He is—how great, how mighty.

But I read nothing of salvation in creation. The rocks tell me, "Salvation is not in us;" the winds howl, but they howl not salvation: the waves rush upon the shore, but among the wrecks which they wash up, the reveal no trace of salvation; the fathomless caves of ocean bear pearls, but they bear no pearls of Grace; the starry heavens have their flashing meteors, but they have no voices of salvation. I find salvation written nowhere, till in this volume of my Father's Grace I find his blessed love unfolded towards the great human family, teaching them that they are lost, but that He can save them, and that in saving them He can be "just, and yet the justifier of the ungodly."

Salvation, then, is to be found *in the Scriptures*, and in the Scriptures only; for we can read nothing of it elsewhere. And while it is to be found only in Scripture, I hold that the peculiar doctrine of revelation is salvation. I believe that the Bible was sent not to teach me history, but to teach me Grace—not to give me a system of philosophy, but to give me a system of divinity—not to teach worldly wisdom, but spiritual wisdom. Hence I hold all preaching of philosophy and science in the pulpit to be altogether out of place. I would check no man's liberty in this matter, for God only is the Judge of man's conscience; but it is my firm opinion that if we profess to be Christians, we are bound to keep to Christianity; if we profess to be Christian ministers, we drivel away the Sabbath day, we mock our hearers, we insult God, if we deliver lectures upon botany, or geology, instead of delivering sermons on salvation. He who does not *always* preach the Gospel should not to be called a true-called minister of God.

Well, then it is salvation I desire to preach to you. We have, in our text, two or three things. In the first place, we are told who they are who will be saved, that is, "them that come into God by Jesus Christ." In the second place we are told the extent of the Savior's ability to save, "He is able to save to the uttermost." And, in the third place, we have the reason given why He can save, "seeing He ever liveth to make intercession for them."

THOSE WHO ARE TO BE SAVED

First, we are told *the people who are to be saved.* And the people who are to be saved are "those who come unto God by Jesus Christ." There is no limitation here of sect or denomination: it does not say, the Baptist, the Independent, or the Episcopalian that come unto God by Jesus Christ, but it simply says, "them," by which I understand men of all creeds, men of all ranks, men of all classes, who do but come to Jesus Christ. They shall be saved, whatever their apparent position before men, or whatever may be the denomination to which they have linked themselves.

1. Now, I must have you notice, in the first place, where these people come to. They "come unto God." By coming to God we are not to understand the mere formality of devotion, since this may be but a solemn means of sinning.

What a splendid general confession is that in the Church of England Prayer Book:

"We have erred and strayed from thy ways like lost sheep; we have done those things which we ought not to have done, and we have left undone those things which we ought to have done, and there is no health in us."

180

There is not to be found a finer confession in the English language. And yet how often, my dear Friends, have the best of us mocked God by repeating such expressions verbally, and thinking we have done our duty?! How many of you go to chapel, and must confess your own absence of mind while you have bowed your knee in prayer, or uttered a song of praise?! My Friends, it is one thing to go to church or chapel; it is quite another thing to go to God. There are many people who can pray right eloquently, and who do so; who have learned a form of prayer by heart, or, perhaps, use an extemporary form of words of their own composing: but who, instead of going to God, are all the while going from God.

Let me persuade you all not to be content with mere formality. There will be many damned who never broke the Sabbath, as they thought, but who, all their lives were Sabbath-breakers. It is as much possible to break the Sabbath in a church as it is to break the Sabbath in the park; it is as easy to break it here in this solemn assembly as in your own houses. Every one of you virtually break the Sabbath when you merely go through a round of duties, having done which, you retire to your chambers, fully content with yourselves, and fancy that all is over—that you have done your day's work—whereas, you have never come to God at all, but have merely come to the outward ordinance and to the visible means, which is quite another thing from coming to God Himself.

And let me tell you, again, that coming to God is not what some of you suppose—now and then sincerely performing an act of devotion, but giving to the world the greater part of your life. You think that if sometimes you are sincere, if now and then you put up an earnest cry to Heaven, God will accept you; and though your life may be still worldly, and your desires still carnal, you suppose that for the sake of this occasional devotion God will be pleased, in His infinite mercy, to blot out your sins. I tell you, sinners, there is no such thing as bringing half of yourselves to God, and leaving the other half away. If a man has come here, I suppose he has brought his whole self with him; and so if a man comes to God, he cannot come, half of him, and half of him stay away. Our whole being must be surrendered to the service of our Maker. We must come to him with an entire dedication of ourselves, giving up all we are, and all we ever shall be, to be thoroughly devoted to his service, otherwise we have never come to God aright.

I am astonished to see how people in these days try to love the world and love Christ too; according to the old proverb, they "hold with the hare and run with the hounds." They are real good Christians sometimes, when they think they ought to be religious; but they are right bad fellows at other seasons, when they think that religion would be a little loss to them. Let me warn you all. It is of no earthly use for you to pretend to be on two sides of the question. "If God be God, serve Him; if Baal be God, serve him." I like an out-and-out man of any sort. Give me a man that is a sinner: I have some hope for him when I see him sincere in his vices, and open to acknowledging his own character; but if you give me a man who is half-hearted, who is not quite bold enough to be all for the devil, nor quite sincere enough to be all for Christ, I tell you, I despair of such a man as that. The man who wants to link the two together is in an extremely hopeless case.

Do you think, sinners, you will be able to serve two masters, when Christ has said you cannot? Do you fancy you can walk with God and walk with mammon too? Will you take God on one arm, and the devil on the other? Do you suppose you can be allowed to drink the cup of the Lord, and the cup of Satan at the same time? I tell you, ye shall depart, as cursed and miserable hypocrites, if so you come to God. God will have the whole of you come, or else you shall not come at all. The whole man must seek after the Lord; the whole soul must be poured out before him;

otherwise it is not acceptable coming to God at all. Oh, halters between two opinions, remember this and tremble.

I think I hear one say, "Well, then, tell us what it is to come to God."

I answer, coming to God implies, leaving something else. If a man comes to God, he must leave his sins; he must leave his righteousness; he must leave both his bad works and his good ones, and come to God, leaving them entirely.

Again, coming to God implies, there is no aversion towards him; for a man will not come to God while he hates God; he will be sure to keep away. Coming to God signifies having some love toward God. Again, coming to God signifies desiring God, desiring to be near to him. And, above all, it signifies praying to God and putting faith in him. This is coming to God; and those that have come to God in that fashion are among the saved. They come to God; that is the place to which their eager spirits hasten.

2. But notice, next, how they come. They "come unto God by Jesus Christ." We have known many persons who call themselves natural religionists. They worship the God of nature, and they think that they can approach God apart from Jesus Christ. There be some men we what of who despise the mediation of the Savior, and, who, if they were in an hour of peril, would put up their prayer at once to God, without faith in the Mediator.

Do such of you fancy that you will be heard and saved by the great God your Creator, apart from the merits of his Son? Let me solemnly assure you, in God's most holy name, there never was a prayer answered for salvation, by God the Creator, since Adam fell, without Jesus Christ the Mediator. "No man can come unto God but by Jesus Christ;" and if any one of you deny the Divinity of Christ, and if any soul among you do not come to God through the merits of a Savior, bold fidelity obliges me to pronounce you condemned persons; for however amiable you may be, you cannot be right in the rest, unless you think rightly of him.

I tell you, you may offer all the prayers that ever may be prayed, but you shall be damned, unless you put them up through Christ. It is all in vain for you to take your prayers and carry them yourself to the throne. "Get thee hence, sinner; get thee hence," says God; "I never knew thee. Why didst not thou put thy prayer into the hands of a Mediator? It would have been sure of an answer. But as thou presentest it thyself, see what I will do with it!" And he read your petition, and casts it to the four winds of Heaven; and thou goest away unheard, unsaved. The Father will never save a man apart from Christ; there is not one soul now in Heaven who was not saved by Jesus Christ; there is not one who ever came to God aright, who did not come through Jesus Christ. If you would be at peace with God, you must come to Him through Christ, as the Way, the Truth, and the Life, making mention of His righteousness, and of His *only*.

3. But when these people come, what do they come for? There are some who think they come to God, who do not come for the right thing. Many a young student cries to God to help him in his studies; many a merchant comes to God that he may be guided through a dilemma in his business. They are accustomed, in any difficulty, to put up some kind of prayer which, if they knew its value, they might cease from offering, for "the sacrifice of the wicked is an abomination to the Lord."

But the poor sinner, in coming to Christ, has only one object. If all the world were offered to him, he would not think it worth his acceptance if he could not have Jesus Christ. There is a poor man, condemned to die, locked up in the condemned cell: the bell is tolling: he will soon be taken off to die on the gallows. There, man, I have brought you a fine robe. What! Not smile at it? Look! It is stiff with silver! Mark you not how it is bedizened with jewels? Such a robe as that cost many and many a pound, and much fine workmanship was expended on it. Contemptuously he smiles at it!

See here, man, I present you something else: here is a glorious estate for you, with broad acres, fine mansions, parks and lawns; take that title deed, 'tis thine. What! Not smile, sir? Had I given that estate to any man who walked the street, less poor than thou art, he would have danced for very joy. And will not you afford even a smile, when I make you rich and clothe you with gold? Then let me try once more.

There is Caesar's purple for you; put it on your shoulders—there is his crown; it shall sit on no other head but thine. It is the crown of empires that know no limit. I'll make thee a king; thou shalt have a kingdom upon which the sun shall never set; thou shalt reign from pole to pole. Stand up; call thyself Caesar. Thou art emperor. What! No smile? What dost thou want? "Take away that bauble," says he of the crown; "rend up that worthless parchment; take away that robe; ay, cast it to the winds. Give it to the kings of the earth who live; but I have to die, and of what use are these to me? Give me a pardon, and I will not care to be a Caesar. Let me live a beggar, rather than die a prince."

So is it with the sinner when he comes to God: he comes for salvation. He says—

> "Wealth and honor I disdain;
>> Earthly comforts, Lord, are vain,
> These will never satisfy,
>> Give me Christ, or else I die."

Mercy is his sole request. Oh my friends, if you have ever come to God, crying out for salvation, and for salvation only, then you have come unto God aright. It were useless then to mock you. You cry for bread: should I give you stones? You would but hurl them at me. Should I offer you wealth? It would be little. We must preach to the sinner who comes to Christ, the gift for which he asks—the gift of salvation by Jesus Christ the Lord—as being his own by faith.

4. One more thought upon this coming to Christ. In what style do these persons come? I will try and give you a description of certain persons, all coming to the gate of mercy, as they think, for salvation. There comes one, a fine fellow in a coach and six! See how hard he drives, and how rapidly he travels; he is a fine fellow: he has men in livery, and his horses are richly caparisoned; he is rich, exceeding rich. He drives up to the gate, and says,

> "Knock at that gate for me; I am rich enough, but still I dare say it would be as well to be on the safe side; I am a very respectable gentleman; I have enough of my own good works and my own merits, and this chariot, I dare say, would carry me across the river death, and land me safe on the other side; but still, it is fashionable to be religious, so I will approach the gate. Porter! Undo the gates, and let me in; see what an honorable man I am."

You will never find the gates undone for that man; he does not approach in the right manner. There comes another; he has not quite so much merit, but still he has some; he comes walking along, and having leisurely marched up, he cries,

> "Angel! Open the gate to me; I am come to Christ: I think I should like to be saved. I do not feel that I very much require salvation; I have always been a very honest, upright, moral man; I do not know myself to have been much of a sinner; I have robes of my own; but I would not mind putting Christ's robes on; it would not hurt me. I may as well have the wedding garment; then I can have mine own too."

186

Ah! The gates are still hard and fast, and there is no opening of them. But let me show you the right man. There he comes, sighing and groaning, crying and weeping all the way. He has a rope on his neck, for he thinks he deserves to be condemned. He has rags on him; he comes to the heavenly throne; and when he approaches mercy's gate he is almost afraid to knock. He lifts up his eyes and he sees it written, "Knock, and it shall be opened to you;" but he fears lest he should profane the gate by his poor touch; he gives at first a gentle rap, and if mercy's gate open not, he is a poor dying creature; so he gives another rap, then another and another; and although he raps times without number, and no answer comes, still he is a sinful man, and he knows himself to be unworthy; so he keeps rapping still; and at last the good angel smiling from the gate, says,

"Ah! This gate was built for beggars not for princes; Heaven's gate was made for spiritual paupers, not for rich men. Christ died for sinners, not for those who are good and excellent. Hoe came into the world to save the vile. 'Not the righteous—sinners, Jesus came to call.' Come in, poor man! Come in. Thrice welcome!"

And the angels sing, "Thrice welcome!" How many of you, dear Friends, have come to God by Jesus Christ in that fashion? Not with the pompous pride of the Pharisee, not with the insincerity of the good man who thinks he deserves salvation, but with the sincere cry of a penitent, with the earnest desire of a thirsty soul after living water, panting as the thirsty heart in the wilderness after the water-brooks, desiring Christ as they that look for the morning; I say, more than they that look for the morning. As my God who sits in Heaven liveth, if you have not come to God in this fashion, you have not come to God at all; but if you have thus come to God, here is the glorious word for you—"He is able to save to the uttermost them that come unto God by him."

THE MEASURE OF THE SAVIOR'S ABILITY

Thus we have disposed of the first point, the coming to God; and now, secondly, *what is the measure of the Savior's ability?* This is a question as important as if it were for life or death—a question as to the ability of Jesus Christ. How far can salvation go? What are its limits and its boundaries? Christ is a Savior: how far is He able to save? He is a Physician: to what extent will His skill reach to heal diseases? What a noble answer the text gives! "He is able to save to the uttermost."

Now, I will certainly affirm, and no one can deny it, that no one here knows how far the uttermost is. David said, if he took the wings of the morning, to fly to the uttermost parts of the sea, even there should God reach him. But who knoweth where the uttermost is? Borrow the angel's wing, and fly far, far beyond the most remote star: go where wing has never flapped before, and where the undisturbed ether is as serene and quiet as the breast of Deity itself; you still, beyond the bounds of creation, where space itself falls, and where chaos takes up its reign: you will not come to the uttermost. It is too far for mortal intellect to conceive of; it is beyond the range of reason or of thought. Now, our text tells us that Christ is "able to save to the uttermost."

1. Sinner, I shall address you first; and saints of God, I shall address you afterwards. Sinner, Christ is "able to save to the uttermost;" by which we understand that the uttermost extent of guilt is not beyond the power of the Savior. Can anyone tell what is the uttermost amount to which a

man might sin? Some of us conceive that Palmer[1] has gone almost to the uttermost of human depravity; we fancy that no heart could be much more vile than that which conceived a murder so deliberate, and contemplated a crime so protracted; but I can conceive it possible that there might be even worse men than he, and that if his life were spared, and he were set at large, he might become even a worse man than he is now. Indeed, supposing he were to commit another murder, and then another, and another, would he have gone to the uttermost? Could not a man be yet more guilty? As long as ever he lives, he may become more guilty than he was the day before. But yet my text says, Christ is "able to save to the uttermost."

I may imagine a person has crept in here, who thinks himself to be the most loathsome of all beings, the most condemned of all creatures. "Surely," says he, "I have gone to the utmost extremity of sin; none could outstrip me in vice." My dear Friend, suppose you had gone to the uttermost, remember that even then you would not have gone beyond the reach of divine mercy; for he is "able to save to the uttermost," and it is possible that you yourself might go a little further, and, therefore, you have not gone to the uttermost yet. However far you may have gone—if you have gone to the very artic regions of vice, where the sun of mercy seems to scatter but a few oblique rays, there can the light of salvation reach you.

If I should see a sinner staggering on in his progress to Hell, I would not give him up, even when he had advanced to the last stage of iniquity. Though his foot hung trembling over the very verge of perdition, I would

---

[1] William Palmer (1824-1856) was also known by the moniker, "the Prince of Poisoners." Palmer was an English doctor who was convicted of murdering his friend John Cook with strychnine and suspected in the deaths of his wife, brother, mother-in-law, and four children. Palmer garnered large sums of money from the deaths of his family, which he later lost through gambling.

not cease to pray for him; and though he should in his poor drunken wickedness go staggering on till one foot were over Hell, and he were ready to perish, I would not despair of him. Till the pit had shut her mouth upon him I would believe it still possible that divine Grace might save him.

See here! He is just upon the edge of the pit, ready to fall; but before he falls, free Grace bids, "Arrest that man!" Down mercy comes, catches him on her broad wings, and he is saved, a trophy of redeeming love. If there be any such in this vast assembly—if there be any here of the outcast of society, the vilest of the vile, the scum, the draff of this poor world—oh! ye chief of sinners! Christ *is* "able to save to the uttermost." Tell that everywhere, in every garret, in every cellar, in every haunt of vice, in every kennel of sin; tell it everywhere! "To the uttermost!" That, "He is able to save them to the uttermost."

2. Yet again: not only to the uttermost of crime, but to the uttermost of rejection. I must explain what I mean by this. There are many of you here who have heard the Gospel from your youth up. I see some here, who like myself are children of pious parents. There are some of you upon whose infant forehead the pure heavenly drops of a mother's tears continually fell; there are many of you here who were trained up by one whose knee, whenever it was bent, was ever bent for you, her first-born son. Your mother has gone to Heaven, it may be, and all the prayers she ever prayed for you are as yet unanswered. Sometimes you wept. You remember well how she grasped your hand, and said to you, "Ah! John, you will break my heart by this your sin, if you continue running on in those ways of iniquity: oh! if you did but melt, and you would fly to Christ."

Do you not remember that time? The hot sweat stood upon your brow, and you said—for you could not break her heart—"Mother, I will think of it;" and you did think of it; but you met your companion outside, and it was all gone: your mother's expostulation was brushed away; like the thin cobwebs of the gossamer, blown by the swift north wind, not a trace of it was left. Since then you have often stepped in to hear the minister.

Not long ago you heard a powerful sermon; the minister spoke as though he were a man just started from his grave, with as much earnestness as if he had been a sheeted spirit come back from the realms of despair, to tell you his own awful fate, and warn you of it. You remember how the tears rolled down your cheeks while he told you of sin, of righteousness, and of judgment to come; you remember how he preached to you Jesus and salvation by the cross, and you rose up from your seat in that chapel, and you said, "Please God I am spared another day, I will turn to Him with full purpose of heart."

And there you are, still unchanged—perhaps worse than you were; and you have spent your Sunday afternoon the angel knows where: and your mother's spirit knows where you have spent it too, and could she weep, she would weep over you who have this day despised God's Sabbath, and trampled on his Holy Word. But do you feel in your heart tonight the tender motions of the Holy Spirit? Do you feel something saying, "Sinner! Come to Christ now?" Do you hear that conscience whispering to you, telling you of your past transgression? And is there some sweet angelic voice, saying, "Come to Jesus, come to Jesus; He will save you yet?"

I tell you, sinner, you may have rejected Christ to the very uttermost; but he is *still able* to save you. There are a thousand prayers on which you have trampled, there are a hundred sermons all wasted on you, there are thousands of Sabbaths which you have thrown away; you have rejected Christ, you have despised His Spirit; but still He ceases not to cry, "Return, return!" He is "able to save thee to the uttermost," if you come unto God by Him.

3. There is another case which demands my particular attention tonight. It is that of the man who has gone to the uttermost of despair. There are some poor creatures in the world, who from a course of crime have become hardened, and when at last aroused by remorse and the pricklings of conscience, there is an evil spirit which broods over them, telling them it is hopeless for such as they are to seek salvation. We have met with some who have gone so far that they have thought that even devils might be saved rather than they could. They have given themselves up for lost, and signed their own death-warrant, and in such a state of mind have positively taken the halter in their hand, to end their unhappy lives.

Despair has brought many a man to a premature death; it has sharpened many a knife, and mingled many a cup of poison. Have I a despairing person here? I know him by his somber face and downcast looks. He wishes he were dead, for he thinks that Hell itself could be scarce worse torment than to be here expecting it. Let me whisper to him words of consolation. Despairing soul! hope yet, for Christ "is able to save to the uttermost;" and though thou art put in the lowest dungeon of the castle of despair, though key after key hath been turned upon thee, and the iron grating of thy window forbids all filing, and the height of thy prison-wall is so awful that thou couldst not expect to escape, yet let me tell thee, there is one at the gate who can break every bolt, and undo every lock; there is one who can lead thee out to God's free air and save thee yet, for though the worst may come to the worst, he "is able to save thee to the uttermost."

4. And now a word to the saint, to comfort him: for this text is his also. Beloved brother in the gospel! Christ is able to save thee to the uttermost. Art thou brought very low by distress? Hast thou lost house and home, friend and property? Remember, thou hast not come "to the uttermost" yet, badly off as you are, thou mightest be worse. He is able to

save thee; and suppose it should come to this, that thou hadst not a rag left, nor a crust, nor a drop of water, still he would be able to save thee, for "He is able to save to the uttermost." So with temptation. If thou shouldst have the sharpest temptation with which mortal was ever tried, He is able to save thee. If thou shouldst be brought into such a predicament that the foot of the devil should be upon thy neck, and the fiend should say, "Now I will make an end of thee," God would be able to save thee then. Ay, and in the uttermost infirmity shouldst thou live for many a year, till thou art leaning on thy staff, and tottering along thy weary life, if thou shouldst outlive Methusaleh, thou couldst not live beyond the uttermost, and He would save thee then. Yes, and when thy little bark is launched by death upon the unknown sea of eternity, He will be with thee; and though thick vapors of gloomy darkness gather round thee, and thou canst not see into the dim future, though thy thoughts tell thee that thou wilt be destroyed, yet God will be "able to save thee to the uttermost."

Then, my Friends, if Christ is able to save a Christian to the uttermost, do you suppose He will ever let a Christian perish? Wherever I go, I hope always to bear my hearty protest against the most accursed doctrine of a saint's falling away and perishing. There are some ministers who preach that a man may be a child of God (now, angels! do not hear what I am about to say, listen to me, ye who are down below in Hell, for it may suit you) that a man may be a child of God today, and a child of the devil tomorrow; that God may acquit a man, and yet condemn him— save him by Grace, and then let him perish—suffer a man to be taken out of Christ's hands, though he has said such a thing shall never take place. How will you explain this? It certainly is no lack of power. You must accuse Him of a want of love, and will you dare to do that? He is full of love; and since He has also the power, He will never suffer one of His people to perish. It is true, and ever shall be true, that He will save them to the very uttermost.

WHY IS JESUS ABLE TO SAVE TO THE UTTERMOST?

Now, in the last place, *why is it that Jesus Christ is "able to save to the uttermost?"* The answer is, that He "ever liveth to make intercession for them." This implies that He died, which is indeed the great source of His saving power. Oh! How sweet it is to reflect upon the great and wondrous works which Christ hath done, whereby He hath become "the high priest of our profession," able to save us! It is pleasant to look back to Calvary's hill, and to behold that bleeding form expiring on the tree; it is sweet, amazingly sweet, to pry with eyes of love between those thick olives, and hear the groanings of the Man who sweat great drops of blood.

Sinner, if thou askest me how Christ can save thee, I tell thee this— He can save thee, because He did not save Himself; He can save thee, because He took thy guilt and endured thy punishment. There is no way of salvation apart from the satisfaction of divine justice. Either the sinner must die, or else someone must die for him. Sinner, Christ can save thee, because, if thou comest to God by Him, then He died for thee. God has a debt against us, and He never remits that debt; He will have it paid. Christ pays it, and then the poor sinner goes free.

And we are told another reason why He is able to save: not only because He died, but because He lives to make intercession for us. That Man who once died on the cross is alive; that Jesus who was buried in the tomb is alive. If you ask me what He is doing; I bid you listen. Listen, if you have ears! Did you not hear Him, poor penitent sinner? Did you not hear His voice, sweeter than harpers playing on their harps? Did you not hear a charming voice? Listen! What did it say? "Oh my Father! Forgive—!"

Why, he mentioned *your* own name! "Oh my Father, forgive him; he knew not what he did. It is true he sinned against light, and knowledge, and warnings; sinned willfully and woefully; but, Father, forgive him!"

Penitent, if thou canst listen, thou wilt hear Him praying for thee. And that is why He is able to save.

A warning and a question, and I will be done. First, *a warning*. Remember, there is a limit to God's mercy. I have told you from the Scriptures, that "He is able to save to the uttermost;" but there is a limit to His purpose to save. If I read the Bible rightly, there is one sin which can never be forgiven. It is the sin against the Holy Spirit. Tremble, unpardoned sinners, lest ye should commit that. If I may tell you what I think the sin against the Holy Spirit is, I must say that I believe it to be different in different people; but in many persons, the sin against the Holy Spirit consists in stifling their convictions. Tremble, my hearers, lest tonight's sermon should be the last you hear. Go away and scorn the preacher, if you like; but do not neglect His warning. Perhaps the very next time thou laughest over a sermon, or mockest at a prayer, or despisest a text, the very next oath thou swearest, God may say, "He is given to idols, let him alone; my Spirit shall no more strive with that man; I will never speak to him again." *That* is the warning.

And now, lastly, the question. Christ has done so much for you: what have you ever done for Him? Ah! Poor sinner, if thou knewest that Christ died for thee—and I know that He did, if thou repentest—if thou knewest that one day thou wilt be His, wouldst thou spit upon Him now? Would thou scoff at God's day, if thou knewest that one day it will be thy day? Would thou despise Christ, if thou knewest that He loves thee now, and will display that love by-and-bye?

Oh! There are some of you that will loathe yourselves when you know Christ because you did not treat Him better. He will come to you one of these bright mornings, and He will say, "Poor sinner, I forgive you;" and you will look up in His face, and say: "What! Lord, forgive me? I used to curse thee, I laughed at thy people, I despised everything that had to do with religion. Forgive me?"

"Yes," says Christ, "give me thy hand; I loved thee when thou hatedst me: come here!"

And sure there is nothing will break a heart half so much as thinking of the way in which you sinned against one who loved you so much.

Oh! Beloved, hear again the text—"He is able to save to the uttermost them that come unto God by him." I am no orator, I have no eloquence; but if I were the one, and had the other, I would preach to you with all my soul. As it is, I only talk right on, and tell you what I do know; I can only say again,

> "He is able;
>   He is willing: doubt no more.
> Come, ye thirsty, come and welcome,
>   God's free bounty glorify:
>
> "True belief and true repentance,
>   Every grace that brings us nigh—
> Without money,
>   Come to Jesus Christ, and buy."

For he is able to save to the uttermost them that come unto God by Him. Oh Lord! Make sinners come! Spirit of God! Make them come! Compel them to come to Christ by sweet constraint, and let not our words be in vain, or our labour lost; for Jesus Christ's sake! Amen.

59374515R00109

Made in the USA
Columbia, SC
02 June 2019